ILLINOIS INSECTS AND SPIDERS

PAINTINGS BY Peggy Macnamara

TEXT BY Division of Insects at the Field Museum

James H. Boone, Paul Z. Goldstein, Chris Grinter, Jim Louderman, Alfred F. Newton, Philip P. Parrillo,

Mary Beth Prondzinski, Margaret K. Thayer, Petra Sierwald, Daniel A. Summers, and John A. Wagner

WITH A FOREWORD BY Maggie Daley

ILLINOIS

INSECTS AND SPIDERS

THE UNIVERSITY OF CHICAGO PRESS

IN ASSOCIATION WITH THE FIELD MUSEUM

CHICAGO AND LONDON

PEGGY MACNAMARA is adjunct associate professor
at the School of the Art Institute; artist-in-residence
and associate of the zoology department at the Field
Museum; instructor at the Field Museum, Chicago
Public Libraries Nature Connection, and Art Institute Family Programs; and the author of *Painting
Wildlife in Watercolor*.

The University of Chicago Press, Chicago 60637
The University of Chicago Press, Ltd., London
© 2005 by The University of Chicago
All rights reserved. Published 2005
Printed in China

14 13 12 11 10 09 08 07 06 05   1 2 3 4 5

ISBN 0-226-50100-0 (paper)

♾ The paper used in this publication meets the
minimum requirements of the American National
Standard for Information Sciences — Permanence
of Paper for Printed Library Materials,
ANSI Z39.48–1992.

Library of Congress Cataloging-in-Publication Data
Macnamara, Peggy.
    Illinois insects and spiders / paintings by Peggy
Macnamara ; text by members of the Division of
Insects at the Field Museum, James H. Boone . . .
[et al.]
        p.   cm.
    ISBN 0-226-50100-0 (cloth : alk. paper)
    1. Insects — Illinois. 2. Spiders — Illinois
3. Insects — Illinois — Pictorial works. 4. Spiders —
Illinois — Pictorial works. I. Boone, James H.
II. Title
    QL475.I3M33 2005
    595.7′09773 — dc22   2004019728

CONTENTS

FOREWORD

Maggie Daley
FIRST LADY OF CHICAGO

The Midwest is a place of diverse beauty and Chicago is no exception—in fact it holds many treasures, some hidden in our own backyards. *Illinois Insects and Spiders* brings art and science together to help readers realize the exotic beauty of the local insect population.

Let this book be your guide as you explore the world of these tiny creatures. Some are predators, others are parasites; some hide in plain sight while others flash a colorful warning. As you page through this book, think about the beautiful and unique insects and spiders that are in your own yard, neighborhood park, or forest preserve and how they affect our world.

Enjoy!

PREFACE

John McCarter

PRESIDENT OF THE FIELD MUSEUM

The museum's mission to educate, research, discover, and conserve the treasures of natural history is complex and extensive. Much of what is being accomplished in the museum occurs away from the public view. The museum exhibition spaces reflect some of what goes on here. Our "Behind the Scenes" tour gives further insight into all the research, educational, and conservation work being done at the Field Museum. *Illinois Insects and Spiders* is another example of work being done on the third and fourth floor making its way down to the public arena. This readable guide is meant to pique your interest in your local population of insects, inspire budding entomologists, and expose the beauty of the local population, as well as provide a clear example of the museum's educational goals. Readable text provided by curatorial staff at the museum accompanies artwork meant to unveil treasures found here at home, where conservation begins.

INTRODUCTION

Peggy Macnamara
ARTIST

After painting watercolors at the Field Museum for more than twenty years, I was unexpectedly given the opportunity to concentrate on insects. I had painted from the museum's vast collection of artifacts, birds, and mammals, as well as its architecture, yet had not paid much attention to the largest group of animals—insects—many of them tucked away in drawers hidden from public view. For the watercolors in this book, I worked from the Field Museum's insect collection and Jim Louderman's personal collection of local insects.

I became uneasy when I learned that I would need to use a microscope to observe and draw the insects in detail. I was accustomed to looking at my subjects directly, holding my pencil a couple of feet from the subject and closing one eye, thus observing how each part related to every other. This system was my mainstay. In this new endeavor, however, I would be leaning over a microscope, unable to see my 20 x 30 inch paper at the

same time. My worries were quickly replaced by excitement. When I sat down and looked through the lens, I saw such a strange figure that my heart began to beat faster. A hairy little alien (a spider) was looking back at me with many eyes! Amazed by its body's outrageous colors and patterns, I felt lost, silly in love. I began drawing forms I had never seen before, gradually forgetting my old methods and creating new ones.

I was also forced to change my palette to accommodate insects. I needed to use more fluorescent and bright colors as well as earth tones made up of layered opposites and metallics. Later, when I took the revised palette outside, my landscapes improved. In a sense, by observing nature's least obvious creature, I began to understand how to paint her showier productions such as skies and mountains. How odd that the smallest things in nature would help me describe the most grand.

Insects as "artist-actors" soon fascinated me. By impersonating the habitats around them, they literally draw their surroundings on themselves in order to blend in. Moths become leaves, beetles become bark, and false eyes are everywhere. Their reflective surfaces distort form and help them disappear. They appear light where a shadow would otherwise make them dark and obviously round. As if using good drawing practices, insects dissolve their form rather than make it obvious.

The experience of painting insects has also afforded me the chance to collect insects myself. Insects are in such abundance that no matter how many are collected, the supply does not diminish. I never quite understood the phenomenon of collecting until now. I get to know the insect better after I have seen it alive. Also, I never walk down a street without the possibility of discovering something new. Vigilance has rewarded me with a wonderful collection of Illinois insects.

The history of art has proved that strong work always contains some element of surprise. Coincidentally, the insect world is a parade of surprises. I invite you to look through my lens and discover the power of patient, heartfelt observation—the starting point of both art and science.

How to Use This Book
This book is meant to introduce the beauty, wonder, and diversity of a local population of insects. The specimens are painted true to scale in re-

lation to each other. (A one-inch scale is in the right-hand corner of every plate.) The first two plates contain examples of different insect orders. Starting with plate III, the paintings illustrate the main insect orders: true bugs, grasshoppers and crickets, butterflies, flies, etc. There is endless variety within these groups, as the following pages demonstrate. Although we present just a sampling, the paintings and text are meant to give you a new perspective on insects and pique your interest in the entomological side of the animal kingdom.

It is hoped that the information throughout this book will dispel the commonly held myths that insects are merely pests. They are a necessary part of the ecosystem, where they serve as food for many species of fish, birds, and other animals. Many bees, flies, and beetles are essential for the cross-pollination of plants. Insects pollinate around 40 percent of the world's flowering plants, including many used by humans for food. When enlarged enough to be seen, insects display wondrous colors and composition. They perform many familiar jobs: garbage recyclers, artificial inseminators, architects, artists, soldiers, and team players.

I have found that the insect experience is a prescription for life. I see the value in moving a little slower, looking ever more closely, and finding treasures in the seemingly mundane. Each local population is worth study and admiration, and *where I am is where to begin*.

A NOTE

FROM THE SCIENTISTS AT
the Field Museum

All creatures on Earth belong to the kingdom Animalia. Most of the familiar animals belong to the vertebrates—animals with bones inside and a vertebral column. These animals, including birds and mammals, are large and showy, but there are only about 4,600 mammal species. In contrast, there are over one million species of insects already discovered and named, with many more waiting to be found and described. When faced with such mind-boggling diversity, it is easy to get lost. The system of biological classification helps to keep an overview. In this classification system, organisms of different species are arranged in groups of similar-looking animals that share certain characteristics. For example, all birds and only birds have feathers. The feathers help us to recognize a bird.

All insects have a hard outer skeleton, as do spiders, millipedes, and crabs. Their legs are stiff and jointed. For these two reasons they are all classified

together in the phylum Arthropoda. All insects have six legs, all spiders and their kin have eight legs, and millipedes and centipedes have thirty or more legs. Counting the legs helps scientists to determine the different arthropod groups — insects, spiders, and centipedes and millipedes. Since there are so many six-legged insects, this group is further divided into orders. Many of the orders are familiar to the reader: beetles (order Coleoptera), butterflies (order Lepidoptera), flies (order Diptera), as well as many others.

There are more species of insects than any other animal class on this planet. Beetles, for example, have more than 400,000 species known to science. When a species is discovered, the author who describes the species and the year the description was published are cited after the Latin species name. This book gives the scientific name for each illustrated species, if possible, followed by the author who described it.

PLATES

Crane Fly and Mixed Illinois Insects

Illinois has a rich history in the study of entomology. An early devotee was Benjamin Walsh. In 1838 he moved from England to Henry County, Illinois, where he owned a three-hundred-acre farm near Cambridge, and later moved to Rock Island. After his retirement, Walsh enjoyed the study of entomology. He became the first Illinois state entomologist and continued his study until his death in 1869. Mr. Walsh began a correspondence with an old classmate, Charles Darwin, after *The Origin of Species* was published. He at first did not agree with the hypothesis, but became a complete convert after further study. This relationship was rich and rewarding for both; Darwin commented on Walsh's "vigor of mind" when it came to scientific study and on his study of entomology. Walsh was editor of *The Practical Entomologist*, and later founded *American Entomologist* with Charles Riley in 1868.

As can be seen from this history, there is much to be learned from Illinois insects. This cover plate provides a glimpse of the beauty and diversity of our insect population.

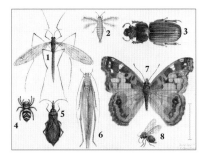

1 **Crane fly.**
Order Diptera, family Tipulidae,
Tipula (unidentified species)

Crane flies are often mistaken for
giant mosquitoes. These primitive
flies are not capable of biting humans; adults feed on nectar and
other plant fluids. The larvae of
Tipula occur in a wide range of habitats from aquatic to most soils. Some
species have become agricultural
pests by devouring seeds and roots of
commercial crops. Aquatic larvae
belong to the guild of shredders that
help to break down leaf packs in
streams. Some primitive four-winged
fossils thought to be related to early
forms of two-winged flies show a
great resemblance to Tipulidae.

2 **Eastern flower thrips.**
Order Thysanoptera, family
Thripidae, *Franklinelliella tritici* (Fitch)

Thrips are an order of minute
insects whose wings resemble straps
with long hairs along their edges.
Biologists have determined that this
wing design reduces aerodynamic
drag, making flight energetically
efficient for tiny insects. Thrips

feed by sucking out the contents of
individual plant cells. They occur on
many kinds of plants as well as in leaf
litter where they feed on fungi. Many
species are of agricultural importance
because they cause direct damage to
plants or serve as vectors of several
viral plant diseases. *Franklinelliella
tritici* and related species are pests of
grasses, trees, and several commercial
crops. They can often be found in the
flower heads of the dandelion.

3 **Bessbug.**
Order Coleoptera, family Passalidae,
Odontotaenius disjunctus (Illiger)

The Bessbug is actually a beetle,
which can easily be found by ripping
apart rotting logs. The passalids have
recently become the subject of research into the origins of insect social
behavior because Bessbugs are known
to exhibit subsocial behavior. Adult
Bessbugs excavate galleries in rotted
wood and tend their developing
young. Studies show that much of the
nutrition that both adults and larvae
derive from their woody diet may
come from the fungi growing in the
wood. Both adults and larvae make
distress sounds through stridulation.

4 Zebra spider.
Order Araneae, family Salticidae (jumping spiders), *Salticus scenicus* (Clerck)

This beautiful little jumping spider is a common guest in the collections of the Field Museum. Like scientists, they work when the sun is up. Their attractive colors complement their eight eyes: four (two of which are large) on the face and two on either side of the carapace. Their amazing leaping power comes from a rapid straightening of the third and fourth pair of legs. They don't build nests.

5 Kissing bug, or cone-nose bug.
Order Hemiptera, family Reduviidae, *Triatoma sanguisuga* (LeConte)

Cone-nose bugs feed on the blood of warm-blooded animals such as rodents and raccoons. Often found in tight-fitting crevices near their hosts, these bugs normally live in wild areas and rarely come into human habitations. Several species of *Triatoma* in Latin America cause enormous human suffering because they act as carriers of Chagas' disease (American trypanosomiasis). Research has shown that *Triatoma* may sometimes carry this pathogen in the United States, but the incidence of that is quite rare.

6 Oblong-winged katydid.
Order Orthoptera, family Tettigoniidae, *Amblycorypha oblongifolia* (DeGeer)

Katydids resort to leaf mimicry as their main strategy for defense. Although green forms dominate in the population, the much rarer yellow and pink color forms are found in some species of *Amblycorypha*. Apparently these color variants are genetically determined. Experiments show that controlling the color of the foliage eaten by these different color forms will not change their final color. The selective advantage of these forms is yet to be determined.

7 Painted lady.
Order Lepidoptera, family Nymphalidae, *Vanessa cardui* (Linnaeus)

The genus *Vanessa* contains several common species that are known to migrate. Populations of *V. cardui* in the eastern United States originate from winter populations in the desert areas of the southwestern United States and northern Mexico. Unlike the monarch butterfly, *V. cardui* does not migrate every year. Periodically, as during El Niño years, these wintering areas become wetter than usual, creating spectacular numbers of painted ladies. Caterpillars feed on thistle, malva, hollyhock, and sunflower. They are covered with urticating spines, which release powerful toxins when touched by humans. The painted lady is notable for having the widest distribution of all butterflies, ranging from North and Central America, Europe, Asia, and Africa.

8 Oak-apple gall wasp.
Order Hymenoptera, family Cynipidae, *Amphibolips confluenta* (Harris)

This small wasp deposits its eggs in the leaves of oak trees, causing a tumor or gall, which is the leaf's response to tissue invasion by a foreign substance. The substances are introduced when the adult deposits its eggs inside the plant or by the metabolites released by a developing larva. The larva benefits from the gall, which serves as a source of both food and protection. The plant receives nothing in return, indicating that this relationship is parasitic.

Life inside a gall is not without its risks. There are many smaller parasitic wasps that specialize in attacking gall-dwelling larvae. Adaptive strategies are constantly being invented by parasites trying to break into galls and by gall-dwellers trying to keep the parasites out. For example, *Neuroterus saltatorius* (Edwards) is another cynipid wasp that makes tiny galls on the underside of oak leaves. These detach from the leaf and fall to the ground. The tiny larva is capable of catapulting the gall into the air when it detects an attack from parasites.

PLATE I

A Mixed Group of Illinois Insects

This plate shows the diversity of Illinois insects. Butterflies and moths, mantids and spiders, fruit flies and beetles — they are all represented. There are insects that are predators and those that are scavengers; they are big and small, colorful and plain. Enjoy the variety of species that inhabit our part of the world.

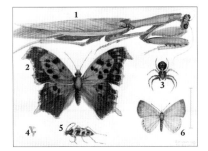

1 **Chinese mantid.**
Order Mantodea, family Mantidae, *Tenodera aridifolia sinensis* Saussure

Mantids comprise an order of insects characterized by powerful raptorial, or grasping, front legs. The word "mantis" is derived from the Greek word for prophet, referring to the prayer-like stance of these insects. A native of China, the Chinese mantid was introduced to the United States for the control of garden pests. Now established, it is one of Illinois' largest and most unusual insects, often measuring 4 1/2 inches long. This species prefers the edges of forests and bushy places where it hunts for insect prey. Mantid females often eat the smaller male while mating. Egg cases are commercially available to control pest insects in gardens, and the young can make an interesting pet for the curious child.

2 **Question mark butterfly.**
Order Lepidoptera, family Nymphalidae, *Polygonia interrogationis* Fabricius

The nymphalid butterflies are known as the brush-footed butterflies because the front legs are reduced in size, lack claws, and are held against the body. Females use them as chemical detectors to locate the correct food plant on which to lay eggs. Nymphalidae comprises the largest family of butterflies. The question mark, named for a silvery pattern on the underside of the hind wing, is a common forest species but often wanders into urban areas. The caterpillars prefer elm, but can also be found on hackberry, basswood, hops, and nettle. Adults feed on ripe fruit, sap flows, and even animal feces.

3 **Goldenrod spider.**
Order Araneida, family Thomisidae,
Misumena vatia (Clerck)

The crab spider does not build a web
for prey capture but waits in flowers
to ambush visiting insects. Males,
as in many other species of spiders,
are much smaller than females. Some
crab spiders are able to change colors
to match their backgrounds. Some
come in pink, white, or yellow forms.
They are most commonly found in
meadows and fields on a variety of
flowers.

4 **Fruit fly.**
Order Diptera, family Drosophilidae,
Drosophila melanogaster (Meigen)

Fruit flies are attracted to the scent
of ripening fruit. Small enough to
crawl through window screens, they
are common house "guests" during
the summer. Their life cycle (about
two weeks) is as short as one would
expect of a species that must pass its
larval stage in something as tempo-
rary as a rotting apple. Its short life
cycle is one reason why the fruit fly
has become the premier experimental animal in the study of genetics.
A mated pair is depicted here.

5 **Long-horned beetle.**
Order Coleoptera, family Cerambycidae, *Typocerus sparsus* LeConte

Cerambycid beetles, which include
some of the largest beetles in the
world, usually have long antennae
and many species are brightly colored. These features make this family
particularly attractive to amateur
collectors. Adult females lay their
eggs on trees and shrubs or the stems
of herbs. Some species may take up
to several years to mature. Children
are often fascinated to discover that
captive adults emit a raspy sound by
stridulating (producing a shrill sound
by rubbing certain body parts).
Adults of *T. sparsus* fly from June
through August. Their larvae feed in
dead pine trees. Adults are often
found taking nectar from flowers.

A recent addition to the Illinois
cerambycid fauna is a notorious tree-
destroying species from China,
Anoplophora glabripennis (Motschul-
sky), dubbed the starry-sky beetle, or
Asian longhorn. The beetle was
accidentally introduced in New York
and Chicago when wooden shipping
pallets made from trees containing
living beetle larvae were imported.
Considering the volume of products
imported into this country every
year, it is a daunting task for Department of Agriculture inspectors to
protect our borders from hitchhiking
pests. Shortly after the media released the story of the beetle invasion in Chicago, a local resident sent
a suspicious-looking beetle to the
Field Museum for identification. The
beetle turned out to be a species of
Apriona, another Asian longhorn on
the short list of tree-destroying
species. It appeared in a shipment
from the company's California plant,
which had originated in China.

6 **Spring azure.**
Order Lepidoptera, family Lycaenidae,
Celastrina ladon (Cramer)

Lycaenid butterflies contain coppers,
blues, and hairstreaks. Most are
small, brightly colored butterflies
that have a white circle of scales
around their eyes. The diminutive
spring azure overwinters as a
chrysalis and emerges in early spring.
Its slug-like larvae feed on flowers.
Ants often protect the caterpillars in
exchange for their honeydew, a sweet
waste product. Adults are common
on flowers in forests and adjacent
areas, and in wooded urban areas.

PLATE II

Different Arthropod Groups

Even the casual observer understands that life in all its diversity presents itself within organized and discrete categories rather than being assembled in willy-nilly fashion. This seems obvious in birds and mammals — birds have feathers and wings while mammals have hair and produce milk. But knowledge of how invertebrate life is organized is less obvious — most terrestrial arthropods are classified as bugs. The gift of curiosity about every critter seems to belong to the very young, and to those eccentric people called biologists and artists.

Arthropods, or creatures with jointed legs, have few qualities that stir human romantic feelings in the way that dogs, cats, or gerbils do. The skin of an arthropod is naked and hard. They seemingly walk on their bellies

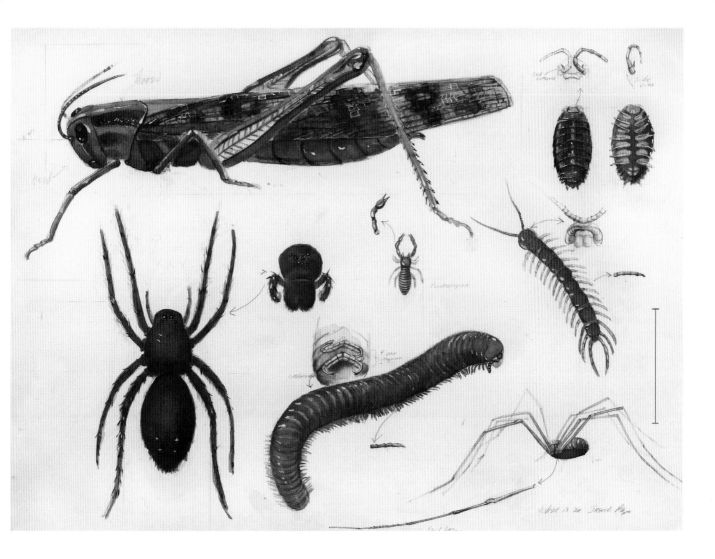

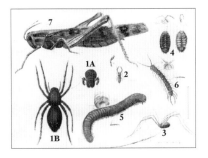

and have too many pairs of legs. Their heads have tiny arms that push food into their mouths and many have bulbous eyes. Their movements are mechanical and in many respects they resemble miniature robots. Yet, in regard to diversity and number, arthropods occupy a preeminent position in the pageant of life. More than 80 percent of the named species on Earth are some kind of arthropod, and the majority of these are insects. Nature's design of the arthropod's body plan is an overwhelming success.

1 **Wolf spider.**
Order Araneae, family Lycosida
(unidentified species)

The major groups of Illinois' terrestrial arthropods can be recognized by observing relatively few body characteristics such as the number of legs, body regions, or the number of antennae. Arthropods that lack antennae, have four pairs of legs, and have chelicerae instead of jaws comprise the class Arachnida. Chelicerae (figure 1A) are appendages at the front of all arachnids. The tip of each chelicera bears a small, claw-like tool, but in the spiders this structure is modified into a piercing fang.

Chelicerate arthropods do not chew their food but are capable of crushing it into a mush into which they spew digestive enzymes. This liquefied broth is then ingested. Spiders, or the order Araneae (figure 1B), comprise the most familiar group of arachnids. They have a waist between their two body regions and spinnerets (silk-producing projections) at the end of their abdomens.

2 **False scorpion.**
Order Pseudoscorpiones
(unidentified species)

The small order Pseudoscorpiones, or false scorpions, consists of tiny creatures that live mostly in leaf litter and look like miniature scorpions without a tail.

3 **Daddy longlegs, or harvestman.**
Order Opiliones, family Phalangiidae,
Odiellus (unidentified species)

The daddy longlegs, or harvestmen, comprise the order Opiliones. They lack the waist of true spiders and do not produce silk. For protection, they lose their legs easily when handled and can release a foul-smelling oil on their attackers.

4 **Roly-poly, or sow bug.**
Order Isopoda, family
Trachelipodidae, *Trachelipus rathkei*

Arthropods that have two pairs of antennae, several pairs of legs, true jaws, and gills on their legs comprise the subphylum Crustacea. The most familiar crustaceans are shrimp and lobsters, but the order Isopoda also contains the familiar roly-poly, or sow bug, which can be found under rocks and logs or even in damp basements. These terrestrial crustaceans have lost their gills and make their living by eating organic matter in the soil.

5 Millipede.
Order Spirobolida, family Spirobolidae, *Narceus americanus* (Beauvois)

The myriapods, meaning *manyleggers*,
consist of two familiar groups—millipedes and centipedes (figure 6). Both
these groups have many body segments and legs, one pair of antennae,
and true jaws. Millipedes have two
pairs of legs on each body segment
and most feed on organic matter
in the soil.

6 Centipede.
Order Lithobiomorpha (unidentified
species)

Centipedes have only a single pair
of legs on each body segment and the
first pair is modified into poisonous
fangs. Centipedes hunt other invertebrates for food.

7 American grasshopper.
Order Orthoptera, family Acrididae,
Schistocerca americana (Drury)

Finally, those arthropods that have
three pairs of legs, a pair of antennae,
and three body regions comprise the
class Hexapoda, meaning *six-leggers*.
These include the insects and their
relatives. The fossil record shows
the first hexapods arose some 400
million years ago (mya) in the lower
Devonian period. Few insect fossils
have been recovered from the inter-
vening geological periods until the
great "Coal Age," or Carboniferous
period, some 325 mya, when a great
flush of winged insects appeared,
including some of the largest insects
ever to exist. The order Protodonata,
extinct primitive dragonflies, attained
wingspans of 71 cm (28 inches) and
palaeodictyopterans, another extinct
order of insects, had wingspans of 56
cm (22 inches). Many examples of
this primitive fauna can be found in
Braidwood, Illinois, in the Mazon
Creek formations. The great mass
extinction of the late Permian period
(245 mya) decimated most of the
Paleozoic insect orders. A remnant
fauna that entered the following
Triassic period evolved into the

modern insects of today. At the
start of the Cretaceous period (145
mya) only about half of the insect
families were similar to those of
today. But by the end of the Cretaceous (65 mya), modern insect families accounted for more than 95
percent of insect diversity.

PLATE III

Metamorphosis

Insect metamorphosis has intrigued humans since antiquity. The ancient Greeks believed that the human soul was released as a butterfly when a person died. In fact, their word *psyche* means both "soul" and "butterfly." Even modern Christians adopted the release of the butterfly from its pupa as a favorite metaphor for conversion and regeneration.

*Simple
Metamorphosis*

*Silverfish
egg*

egg

Metamorphosis

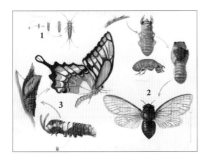

1 **Simple development of a silverfish.**

Order Thysanura, family Lepismatidae (unidentified species)

The developmental types of hexapods fall into three categories. The most primitive hexapods have a simple development (*ametaboly*) in which the young, upon hatching from an egg, are virtually indistinguishable from their adult forms apart from their smaller size. Orders of hexapods with simple development include the Protura, Collembola, Diplura, Thysanura, and Archaeognatha. Ametabolous hexapods are wingless, tend to be small in size, and most are closely associated with soil habitats. With the exception of the Collembola, none of these orders contains many species.

2 **Incomplete metamorphosis of a periodical cicada.**

Order Homoptera, family Cicadidae, *Magicicada tredecim* (Walsh & Riley)

The second developmental type is incomplete metamorphosis (*hemimetaboly*). Here the young are less similar to the adult, often with dramatic differences in color or body ornamentation. The young have external wing buds, which remain inconspicuous until the final molt into the adult. The young of these insects are called *nymphs* in terrestrial forms and *naiads* in aquatic groups. This convention is sometimes ignored and the subadult form may simply be called a "larva." In general, both adults and young of terrestrial hemimetabolous insects occupy the same habitats. Examples of these include the Orthoptera, Blattodea, Hemiptera, Mantodea, and Dermaptera. Aquatic hemimetabolous orders include the Odonata and Ephemeroptera. These orders are diverse in their habits, occur in various types of habitats, and many contain large numbers of species.

3 **Complete metamorphosis of an eastern tiger swallowtail.**
Order Lepidoptera, family Papilion-idae, *Papilio glaucus* Linnaeus

The last developmental type is complete metamorphosis (*holometaboly*) and represents the ultimate form of metamorphosis. A distinct stage, called the *pupa*, is inserted between the last larval instar and the adult.

The larva of holometabolous insects has no external wing buds (these have become internal). Although the pupal stage appears dormant, it is a time of intense metabolic activity with a major reorganization of tissues, organs, and exoskeleton into the adult form. Several advantages can be inferred in the development of this form of metamorphosis. Perhaps the most important benefit is that the larva is an entirely different form than the adult, which allows it to utilize habitats not possible for adults. The most diverse insect orders belong to this group. Common insect orders with complete metamorphosis include Coleoptera, Neuroptera, Trichoptera, Lepidoptera, Diptera, Hymenoptera, and Mecoptera.

PLATE IV

Mimicry

Among nature's many strategies for self-preservation, few are more exquisite than that of mimicry. Mimicry employs the genetic manipulation of structure and color into patterns that resemble other objects in the environment. These patterns, called *models*, become co-opted because they furnish protection from predators. Mimics use a great range of plants and animals as models to imitate. These adaptations involve physical resemblance, and often include modifications in behavior to enhance the disguise. Insects that mimic plants tend to imitate specific parts of plants such as leaves, spines, or twigs, and are motionless. Insects that imitate other insects duplicate the warning coloration of their models in addition to their wing flexing, antennal waving, or other threatening behaviors.

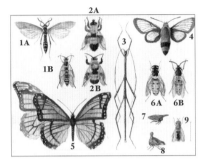

1 **Ash borer, or lilac borer.**
Order Lepidoptera, family Sesiidae,
Podosesia syringae (Harris)

The sesiids, or clearwing moths, have
developed many forms that mimic
the appearance of wasps. *Podosesia
syringae* (figure 1A) bears a striking
resemblance to species of the paper
wasp genus *Polistes* (figure 1B). Adult
moths are active in late spring in time
for lilac blossoms. Females lay their
eggs on the bark of lilac, privet, and
ash. The caterpillars mine tunnels
inside the wood of these plants, and
large populations often kill the host.
The pupa overwinters inside its
gallery and emerges the following
spring.

2 **Robber fly.**
Order Diptera, family Asilidae,
Laphria thoracica (Fabricius)

This species (figure 2A) is virtually
indistinguishable from common
bumble bees (*Bombus*) (figure 2B).
The species is quite variable, having
the abdomen either mostly yellow or
entirely black. Honey bees are among
the favorite food of this predatory fly,
and beekeepers are often mystified to
see "bumble bees" carrying off their
bees. As far as is known, their larvae
feed on soft-bodied insects that live
in soil or rotting stumps.

3 **Walkingstick.**
Order Phasmatodea, family
Heteronemiidae, *Diapheromera
femorata* (Say)

Walkingsticks often astonish children when they see inanimate twigs
walk along the trunk of a tree. This
common Illinois species eats the
leaves of many varieties of trees but
is particularly fond of oaks. Females
drop their eggs to the ground from
their tree-top perches, a phenomenon that sounds like rain when there
is a dense population. After overwintering in the leaf litter, the young
hatch in late spring and feed on
shrubs. Adults look for mates during
late summer and fall. Phasmids are
twig mimics of the trees on which
they feed. When threatened, they
become motionless, and can remain
so for long periods. Although they
may evade detection from visual
hunters such as birds, they play host
to several parasitic wasps and flies.

4 **Snowberry clearwing moth.**
Order Lepidoptera, family Sphingidae, *Hemaris diffinis* (Boisduval)

This day-flying sphinx moth is another mimic of bumble bees. Adults
can be found at the flowers of snowberry, honeysuckle, lilac, and thistles.
Larvae feed on dogbane, snowberry,
and honeysuckle. This species is
often attracted to gardens in urban
areas.

5 **Viceroy butterfly.**
Order Lepidoptera, family Nymphalidae, *Leminitis archippus* (Cramer)

A mimic of the monarch (*Danaus
plexippus* [Linnaeus]), the variable
viceroy also mimics the queen
(*Danaus gilippus* [Cramer]), which
replaces the monarch in southern
states. New research has raised the
question that the viceroy may not be
as palatable as previously thought,
and that it may be the monarch and
queen that benefit from a resemblance to the viceroy. Viceroy caterpillars, which feed on willow and
poplar, are themselves mimics of bird
droppings. Three broods are produced during the year.

6 **Hover fly.**
Order Diptera, family Syrphidae,
Spilomyia hamifera (Loew)

The family Syrphidae contains many
mimics of bees and wasps. The genus
Spilomyia (figure 6A is *S. hamifera*)
includes many convincing mimics of
the yellowjacket genus *Vespula* (figure
6B). They wave their front legs, giving
the appearance of antennae. Adults
are found around flowers, while the
larvae inhabit tree holes and are
cambium-feeders.

7 **Treehopper.**
Order Hemiptera, suborder
Homoptera, family Membracidae,
Campylenchia latipes (Say)

This species tends to feed on the sap
of perennial composite plants (such
as goldenrod) and spends its entire
life on these weeds. Its small (rarely
more than a half inch), thorn-like
body goes unnoticed by visual predators. It does not have many natural
enemies.

8 **Treehopper.**
Order Hemiptera, suborder
Homoptera, family Membracidae,
Glossonotus crataegi (Fitch)

See figure 7 above and plate X for
more information on Homoptera.

9 **Soldier fly.**
Order Diptera, family Stratiomyidae,
Odontomyia cincta (Olivier)

Many soldier flies are also mimics of
wasps. Adults of *O. cincta* are often
found among flowers. Its larvae are
aquatic, feeding on organic matter in
ponds. See plate XIII for more information on flies.

PLATE V

Garden Insects

From beetles to butterflies, and from earwigs to wasps, this is a group of insects commonly found in Illinois gardens and yards.

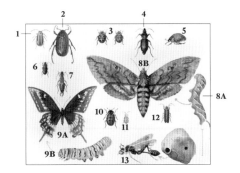

1 Goldenrod leaf beetle.
Order Coleoptera, family Chrysomelidae, *Trirhabda canadensis* (Forster)

Both adults and larvae of *Trirhabda* live in the leaves and flowers of goldenrod. Pupation occurs in the soil. Unlike most other chrysomelids, this beetle overwinters as an egg. As with many herbivores (plant-feeders), *T. canadensis* responds to windborne odor plumes to locate patches of goldenrod. Colonists tend to be picky, rejecting patches that show signs of prior leaf-feeding in favor of more lush patches. Studies indicate that heavy feeding by this beetle can cause Missouri goldenrod to disappear, surviving as dormant rhizomes and reappearing up to thirteen years later.

2 May beetle, or Junebug.
Order Coleoptera, family Scarabaeidae, *Phyllophaga fusca* (Froelich)

These beetles emerge in the spring and can often be found attracted to porch lights. Gardeners are more familiar with their C-shaped, whitish larvae, called "white grubs," which feed on plant roots below the ground. They can do considerable damage to carrot, corn, grass, potato, and tomato plants. Typically, larvae take three years to mature into adults. Christmas tree growers discovered that the grubs of *P. fusca* are fond of Fraser fir trees.

3 **Multicolored Asian lady beetle.**
Order Coleoptera, family
Coccinellidae, *Harmonia axyridis*
(Pallas)

This nonnative species was introduced to the United States to control aphids. Several periods of release took place mostly in the 1980s. The species is now well established and continues to spread its range. It is an effective predator, and research has demonstrated that *H. axyridis* will outcompete and displace some of the Illinois native ladybugs. The species has gained notoriety for its spectacular fall aggregations; in search of tall, highly reflective surfaces, thousands of individuals may land on the side of a building.

4 **Ground beetle.**
Order Coleoptera, family Carabidae,
Pterostichus (Morphonosoma) stygicus
Say

The genus *Pterostichus* is quite diverse in North America and Europe. All are efficient predators and occupy the highest levels in the food chain of their habitat—leaf litter. *Pterostichus stygicus* is a generalist predator, hunting many different kinds of prey occurring both in wooded and open habitats; it may even include plant seeds in its diet. During the day, *P. stygicus* hides under fallen bark, logs, or rocks where moisture conditions are high. It actively searches for prey at night. Larvae appear in late summer and are predators in leaf litter.

5 **Japanese beetle.**
Order Coleoptera, family
Scarabaeidae, *Popillia japonica*
(Newman)

The Japanese beetle was accidentally introduced to New Jersey in 1916 and has been spreading westward ever since. It had established itself in Illinois by the 1980s. This beetle's appetite for more than 400 plant species makes it a particularly destructive pest. The larvae are also destructive, feeding underground on grass roots. Larvae overwinter and emerge as adults in early summer.

The United States Department of Agriculture has made several attempts to control the spread of the Japanese beetle with biological agents. Asian tiphiid wasps (*Tiphia vernalis* Rohwer) were released in the United States in the 1920s and are now established. Around the same time, the tachinid fly (*Istocheta aldrichi* [Mesnil]) was also released. Research indicated that by the 1970s about 20 percent of the beetles tested in Connecticut were being killed by the tachinid fly.

6 **Ground beetle.**
Order Coleoptera, family
Carabidae, *Amara cupreolata*
Putzeys

The genus *Amara* contains many species that live in dry, open areas with sparse vegetation. Many are associated with humans and live in urban habitats such as lawns. *Amara cupreolata* prefers sandy soil and is often found in abandoned lots. These familiar blackish beetles with brassy reflections can often be seen scampering across sidewalks on sunny days.

7 European earwig.
Order Dermaptera, family
Forficulidae, *Forficula auricularia*
Linnaeus

This species is native to Europe and
was first noticed in the United States
in the early 1900s. It is now well
established throughout the United
States. Earwigs tend to be omniv-
rous, taking vegetable and animal
food. Nocturnal in habits, they spend
their days hiding in tight crannies. In
large numbers they can become pests
of some commercial and ornamental
plants.

The earwig myth, like so many
other legends, may be based on
isolated incidents. Due to their habit
of seeking close-fitting crevices in
which to hide, there may be authen-
tic cases where an earwig ventured
into a human ear. This is not, however, their preferred habitat, and if
such cases ever occurred they were
certainly accidental. The only earwigs associated with mammals are a
small group that feeds on the skin
secretions of bats and some rodents.

8 Tomato hornworm.
Order Lepidoptera, family
Sphingidae, *Manduca
quinquemaculata* (Haworth)

Gardeners are often surprised to find
large green caterpillars (figure 8A)
hanging from the stems of their
prized tomatoes. These are called
"hornworms," named for the red
spine that surmounts the end of the
abdomen. When disturbed, the
larvae often raise the front half of the
body with their head and thoracic
legs pulled in, resembling Egyptian
sphinxes. These caterpillars also
readily feed on eggplant, pepper, and
potato plants. Gardeners may notice
white capsules covering the caterpillar's body—these are cocoons of a
parasitic wasp, *Cotesia*. Adult moths
(figure 8B) are rarely seen because of
their nocturnal habits. Their rapid
wing beats emit a low pitched whir
reminiscent of a hummingbird as
they visit evening blossoms for a
midnight meal.

9 Black swallowtail.
Order Lepidoptera, family
Papilionidae, *Papilio polyxenes asterius*
Stoll

The black swallowtail butterfly
(figure 9A) is often found in home
gardens where carrot, dill, parsley, or
fennel is planted. The caterpillars
(figure 9B) eat the foliage, but are
particularly fond of the flowers. A
feature of swallowtail caterpillars is a
forked, yellow-colored gland, called
an *osmeterium*, located directly behind
the head. These glands are eversible
(can be turned inside out) and emit
an odor noxious to birds when the
caterpillar is under attack.

10 Convergent lady beetle.
Order Coleoptera, family
Coccinellidae, *Hippodamia convergens*
Guérin Méneville

Coccinellids are familiar insects to
gardeners because of their predatory
habits. With some exceptions, most
feed on soft-bodied insects such as
aphids. Many have bright colors,
which are used to warn predators
that they produce noxious secretions
if molested. *Hippodamia convergens* is
a common native species throughout
Illinois. Adults overwinter and
emerge in the spring. Females begin
to lay their eggs when aphids first
appear on plants. Larvae spend the
next month searching for prey. They
pupate and produce another generation of adults. In warmer parts of the
United States, two generations can
be produced in a single season.

The convergent's reputation as
an effective predator has led to its
commercial use in pest control.
Insectaries gather large numbers of
the beetle from overwintering aggregations in the western United States
and ship them to gardeners who
desire natural pest control. Torpid
adults that have emerged from their
winter sleep are scripted by nature to

migrate before feeding, a fact often not heeded by suppliers. Gardeners are sometimes horrified to see their newly released ladybug colony fly away, ignoring the plump aphids in front of them.

11 Striped cucumber beetle.
Order Coleoptera, family Chrysomeli-dae, *Acalymma vittata* (Fabricius)

The striped cucumber beetle is one of the most destructive pests to cucumbers, squash, and gourds in the United States. Larvae feed below the ground on small roots or burrow into the main root. Adults attack seedlings and the foliage and shoots of mature plants. They overwinter and lay eggs by early summer. A new generation of adults appears by August.

12 Firefly, or lightning bug.
Order Coleoptera, family Lampyridae, *Photinus pyralis* (Linnaeus)

The lampyrids are soft-bodied beetles with bioluminescent organs in their abdomens. The familiar greenish-yellow flash of *P. pyralis* incites awe in children who spend early summer evenings sweeping them out of the air and imprisoning them in glass jars. The flashes of lampyrids serve to communicate location during courtship. The larvae, commonly called "glowworms," light up the margins of ponds like burning coals. These predatory larvae feed on mollusks, earthworms, and larvae of other insects. Some adults apparently are also predatory, although most species do not feed.

The physiology of firefly bioluminescence is one of the true marvels of nature. Luciferin, a protein in the light organ, is oxidized by an enzyme called *luciferase*. An amazing 99 percent of the energy used in this process is converted into light; in contrast, only 10 percent of the energy used to light an incandescent bulb is converted into light.

13 Mud dauber.
Order Hymenoptera, family Spheci-dae, *Sceliphron caementarium* (Drury)

These wasps can be seen collecting mud at the margins of ponds or in the backyard after the lawn has been watered. A female looks for a secluded space to construct a mud nest. Each nest may have several cylindrical chambers, each of which the wasp fills with a single egg and several paralyzed spiders for food before sealing it.

PLATE VI

Endangered and Threatened Insect Species

The insects depicted on this plate have been designated "endangered" or "threatened" because their numbers have been reduced to small, highly specific remnant populations, usually resulting from loss of habitat. A federally endangered species is in danger of extinction throughout all or a significant portion of its range. A federally threatened species is likely to become an endangered species. Both residential and industrial development and adverse changes in their ecosystems have contributed to this decline. They are often associated with commensally evolved host plants, the disappearance of which has caused the simultaneous elimination of the insects. Many of these species are also desirable to collectors, adding further stress to their already reduced populations if not protected.

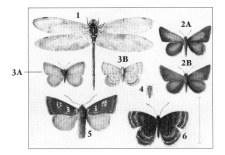

1 **Hine's emerald dragonfly.**
Order Odonata, family Corduliidae,
Somatochlora hineana Williamson

This metallic, gem-like "green-eyed
dragon" lives only in spring-fed
marshes and sedge meadows high in
calcium carbonate based on a substrate of dolomite bedrock. The
larvae spend 2 to 4 years in their
watery nursery, going through numerous molts while feeding on other
aquatic insects, and eventually crawl
on land to shed their final skin and
emerge as an adult dragonfly. Adults
live a short 4 to 5 weeks.

2 **Arogos skipper.**
Order Lepidoptera, family
Hesperiidae, *Atrytone arogos*
(Boisduval & LeConte)

Although often overlooked because
of their generally mousy appearance,
skippers are easily recognized as
belonging in the order Lepidoptera
because they share similarities with
butterflies and moths. This species
requires native grasses, such as big
bluestem, as host plants for its caterpillar stage. With less than 1 percent
of native prairie habitat remaining in
Illinois, it is considered a stray from
eastern populations and exceedingly
rare or localized. Recent discovery
of a cryptic species on the offshore
islands of North Carolina has
prompted studies of the insect's
DNA in order to address conservation status. Figure 2A shows the male,
figure 2B shows the female. Males
perch on low plants near native
grasses to wait for females. Females
deposit eggs one at a time under
leaves.

3 **Karner blue butterfly.**
Order Lepidoptera, family Lycaenidae, *Lycaeides melissa samuelis* (Nabokov)

This attractive "blue" is about 1 inch in wingspan and sexually dimorphic (i.e., males and females differ in appearance). They require wild lupine as a host plant for the larval stage, and the caterpillars are involved in a mutualistic relationship with certain species of ants. The loss of appropriate habitat for these organisms has contributed to the butterfly's demise. Lupine grows in northern sand barrens, pockets of which barely exist in our altered Illinois topography. Although once found in Illinois Beach State Park in Zion, they have not been seen there for a number of years despite restorative lupine plantings. The sand counties of Wisconsin and the Indiana Dunes retain the closest known populations of this species. Figure 3A shows the upperside, 3B shows the underside.

4 **Leafhopper.**
Order Homoptera, family Cicadellidae, *Paraphlepsius lupalus* (Hamilton)

This species is listed as endangered in Illinois. Little is known about the species. Presumably it is a tallgrass prairie specialist. See plate X for more information.

5 **Rattlesnake-master borer moth.**
Order Lepidoptera, family Noctuidae, *Papaipema eryngii* Bird

The genus *Papaipema* contains many species associated with plants of prairie habitats. Eggs are usually laid in the fall on or near the host plant where they pass the winter. Larvae emerge in spring and excavate tunnels in the stem or roots during the summer where they feed on pith. Adult moths emerge in late summer and fall. Larvae are attacked by a number of predators, including rodents and woodpeckers as well as parasitic flies and wasps. The larvae of *P. eryngii* bore into the stems of rattlesnake master. This species occurs in Chicago-area prairies and has recently been discovered in Missouri, Oklahoma, Kentucky, and along the coastal plain of eastern North Carolina.

6 **Swamp metalmark.**
Order Lepidoptera, family Lycaenidae, *Calephelis mutica* (McAlpine)

Another "highly specialized" red-brown butterfly with metallic markings, endemic to bogs, swamps, and wet meadows, *C. mutica* has a single summer brood in our region, relying on swamp thistle and roadside thistle for host plants on which to lay their eggs and feed their larvae. As adults, they prefer the nectar of yellow flowers, such as black-eyed Susans.

PLATE VII

Dragonflies

The Odonata, or "toothed ones," is a very ancient order of insects. They represent some of the earliest forms of flying insects, the Palaeoptera ("old wings"), which are incapable of folding their wings over their backs. Most palaeopteran orders disappeared during the mass extinctions of the Permian period (245 mya) and today only the dragonflies and mayflies (Ephemeroptera) remain. The larvae, or naiads, are aquatic predators on many kinds of stream invertebrates, and those of larger dragonflies even hunt and eat tadpoles and small fish. The larvae have a specialized lower lip (labium) that can suddenly jut out to catch unsuspecting prey nearby.

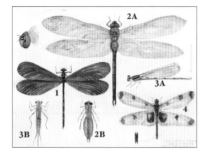

1 **Ebony jewelwing.**
Order Odonata, family Calopterygi-
dae, *Calopteryx maculata* (Beauvois)

Jewelwings (Calopteryx) are some of
the most dazzling Odonata in the
United States. *Calopteryx maculata* is
dimorphic: the male (shown) has a
metallic green body and black wings
while the female is somewhat duller,
has brownish wings and a large white
spot along the front edge of the wing.
They prefer to perch in lush vegetation near streams. Both sexes periodically open and snap shut their wings
to signal where they are. Males en-
gage in territorial dogfights, which
are sometimes fatal.

2 **Green darner.**
Order Odonata, family Aeshnidae,
Anax junius (Drury)

Green darners (figure 2A) are large,
strong, and fast flyers. These "pond-
hawks" migrate into northern Illinois
counties from the south as early as
May and stay on as summer residents.
Voracious predators, large numbers
of darners can be observed flying
in from offshore Lake Michigan
where they have been catching
flies all afternoon. They have sharp
mandibles and can give a painful bite.
Figure 2B shows the larval form.

3 **Familiar bluet.**
Order Odonata, family Coenagrion-
idae, *Enallagma civile* Hagen

The genus *Enallagma*, known as
the "bluets," is Illinois' most diverse
genus of damselflies. Their vernacu-
lar name derives from the dusty
bluish color common in many
species. Adults may be found along
pond margins or in fields near water
(figure 3A). After mating, the female
may spend more than an hour below
the surface of the water depositing
her eggs. The larvae appear to prefer
still or slow-moving bodies of water.
Figure 3B shows the larval form.

4 **Calico pennant.**
Order Odonata, family Libellulidae,
Celithemis elisa (Hagen)

Celithemus is an eastern-endemic
genus of ornate dragonflies in the
United States. Males and females are
similarly patterned. Both start out
with yellow abdomens and wing
markings, but males mature to deep
red markings. Males apparently are
not territorial. Adults can be found
perching on brush and cattails along
the margins of ponds or lakes. Eggs
are laid in water. Larvae overwinter
1 to 2 years in weedy areas of ponds
and lakes, and emerge as naiads in
the spring.

PLATE VIII

Grasshoppers and Roaches

The Orthoptera are a group of large and easily recognized insects, which includes the grasshoppers, crickets, katydids, mole crickets, and camel crickets. The grasshoppers have short antennae and their ears (tympanal organs) are on either side of the first segment of their abdomen, whereas katydids and crickets have long antennae and "ears" on their front legs. The Orthoptera can be found in most habitats and are known for their songs.

Roaches are in the order Blattaria and many common species can be found in the family Blattidae, including the oriental cockroach, American cockroach, and brown roach.

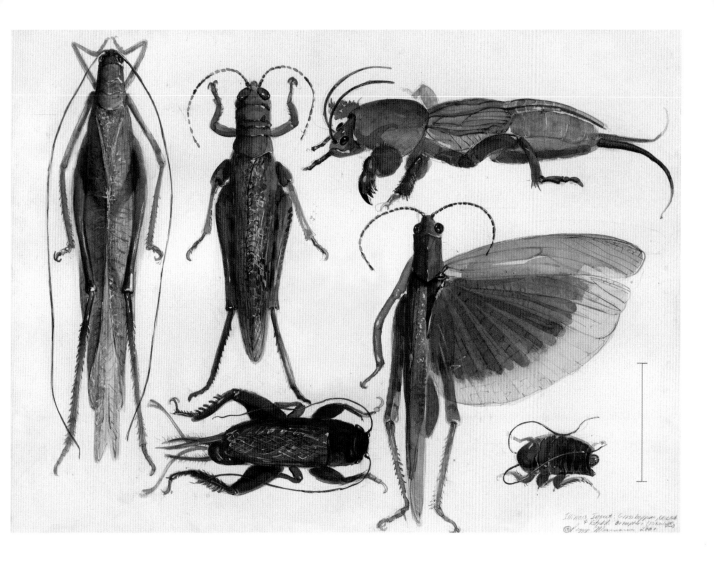

Illinois Insects: Grasshopper, cricket
& Katydid (example of three)
© Peggy Macnamara 2001

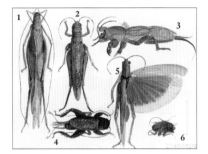

1 **Fork-tailed bush katydid.**
Order Orthoptera, family Tettigoniidae, *Scudderia furcata* Brunner

The tettigoniids, or katydids, are
more familiar to us by their calls than
by their appearance. Most are green
in color and hide in vegetation by
resembling leaves. Although the
majority of katydids eat leaves, some
have adopted carnivorous habits.
Male katydids communicate by
rubbing the bases of their wings
together to produce a raspy "ticking"
sound. *Scudderia furcata* can be heard
in the treetops during late summer
evenings.

The science of audio recording has
progressed beyond the domain of the
birding community and now many
commercial and noncommercial
products are available that feature
the songs of insects. Most Illinois
katydid songs can be found on
several Web sites.

2 **Differential grasshopper.**
Order Orthoptera, family Acrididae,
Melanoplus differentialis (Thomas)

This species appears in great numbers in fields that are turning brown
in the fall. In cultivated areas it can
often become a destructive pest of
crops. It is often found in company
with a smaller, related species, the
red-legged grasshopper, *M. femur-
rubrum* (DeGeer).

The genus *Melanoplus* contains
many species of "spur-throated"
grasshoppers, named for a peg that
juts out between the front legs. Some
of the most economically important
species in the United States belong to
this genus. Perhaps the most notorious is a western species, *Melanoplus
spretus* (Welsh), a scourge to farmers
during the pioneer days. Laura Ingalls
Wilder gives an eyewitness account
of the devastation caused by this
locust ("a grasshopper that swarms")
in her book, *On the Banks of Plum
Creek*. Many farmers gave up in de-
spair and moved away because of
this insect. Surprisingly, this species,
which was the cause of so much
human suffering, came to an enig-
matic end. For reasons yet unclear,
populations of the Rocky Mountain

locust collapsed early in the twentieth century and it is now extinct. A glacier in the Beartooth Mountains of Montana preserves the remains of a swarm of these locusts that occurred over two hundred years ago.

3 **Northern mole cricket.**
Order Orthoptera, family Gryllotalpidae, *Neocurtilla hexadactyla* (Perty)

These crickets are rather mole-like in appearance, with very modified front legs that are adapted for digging through soil. Females of *N. hexadactyla* make long tunnels and excavate side tunnels, which become egg chambers. A single clutch of eggs is produced in the early summer. The nymphs grow and overwinter. By the following summer these nymphs mature, find a mate, and lay eggs the following year.

4 **Northern field cricket.**
Order Orthoptera, family Gryllidae, *Gryllus pennsylvanicus* Burmeister

Gryllidae is a diverse family of Orthoptera commonly known as the crickets. *Gryllus pennsylvanicus* is found throughout Illinois. The cheerful songs of the males attract curious females. The species overwinters in the egg stage and nymphs hatch in May. Adults appear by July and August. They are omnivorous, feeding on plant seeds as well as a variety of insects. Females have long, thin ovipositors through which they lay their eggs in the soil.

5 **Carolina grasshopper.**
Order Orthoptera, family Acrididae, *Dissosteira carolina* (Linnaeus)

The Acrididae comprise the largest family of the Orthoptera. Because their antennae are less than half the length of their bodies, they are commonly known as the short-horned grasshoppers. Most have their "ears" on the sides of their abdomens. Short-horned grasshoppers can pro-duce a raspy call by rubbing their legs over their front wings. The Carolina grasshopper is a familiar species found in open barren areas with sparse vegetation. When approached, it bolts into the air for a short, erratic, and noisy flight.

6 **Brown roach.**
Order Blattodea, family Blattidae, *Periplaneta brunnea* Burmeister (nymph)

Blattids are a family of roaches to which many economically important species belong. Unlike its well known cousin, the American cockroach (*Periplaneta americana* [Linnaeus]), *P. brunnea* makes its living out of doors. Adults can live up to 20 months and can produce up to 30 oothecae (egg capsules) in a week.

PLATE IX

Hemiptera (True Bugs and a Cicada)

Most people tend to call all insects "bugs." To an entomologist, however, a bug is one of many species of the order Hemiptera, which means "half wing." This refers to the fact that part of the first pair of wings is hard, while the rest of the first pair and all of the second pair are membranous (see plate X concerning the Homoptera). Hemipterans also have modified piercing and sucking mouthparts; some suck plant juices and are plant pests, while others can bite painfully. Many true bugs are aquatic.

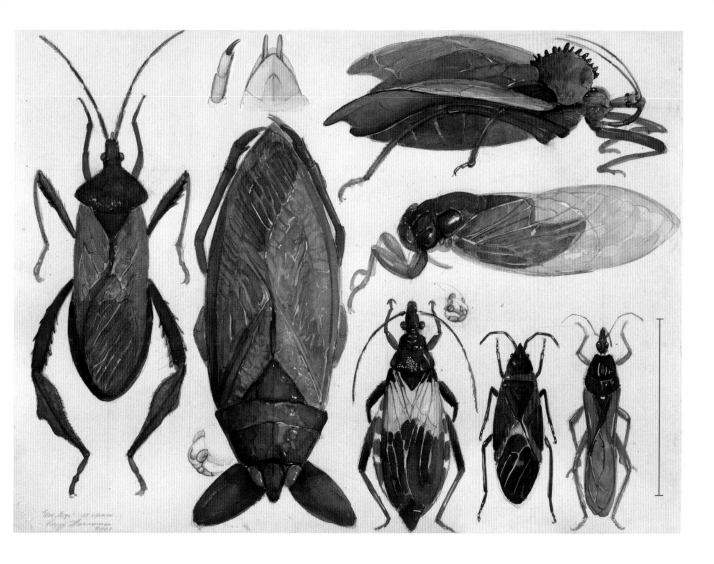

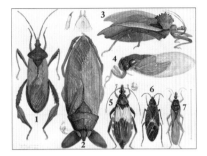

1 **Leaf-footed bug.**
Order Hemiptera, family Coreidae, *Acanthocephala terminalis* (Dallas)

Leaf-footed bugs are medium- to large-sized true bugs that often release a defensive chemical when handled. These oils are generally unpleasant to potential predators and some are powerful lacrimators (cause eyes to tear). They often have expanded hind legs, which give them the nickname of "leaf-footed bugs." *Acanthocephala terminalis*, which is about 3/4 inches (2 cm) long, can be found in meadows and other open areas. Several species are agricultural pests.

2 **Giant water bug, or "toe-biter."**
Order Hemiptera, family Belostomatidae, *Lethocerus* (unidentfied species).

Lethocerus, or the giant water bug, is a large predaceous bug that lives in ponds, lakes, and slow-moving streams. It is among the dominant insects of aquatic habitats. Able to breathe underwater because of a snorkel-like extension at the back of its abdomen (see detail above this figure), the giant water bug hides in the mud and ambushes prey as they swim by, using its raptorial front legs to seize prey often larger than itself. It hunts insects, salamanders, tadpoles, small fish, and snails. It kills its prey by injecting powerful enzymes. Swimmers sometimes complain of being bitten or pinched by the bugs after accidentally stepping on them. Three species can be found in Illinois. These bugs fly from pond to pond during mating season, when they can be seen near electric lights. Larvae are deposited on plants above water.

3 **Wheel bug.**
Order Hemiptera, family Reduviidae, *Arilus cristata* (Linnaeus)

Found in southern Illinois, the wheel bug is distinctive for the toothed crest of its thorax. It is a formidable predator of caterpillars and other insects, and therefore welcomed by farmers.

4 **Periodical cicada.**
Order Hemiptera, family Cicadidae,
Magicicada tredecim (Walsh & Riley)

Most people are familiar with the
loud buzzing call of cicadas during
the dog days of summer. Cicadas are
unusual in that the young have pro-
tracted growth periods; the length
of these periods is species specific.
The nymphs live underground and
pierce plant roots for nourishment,
and then, at periodic intervals,
emerge from the ground to become
a short-lived adult. Periodical cicadas
have the longest life span of all cicadas. *Magicicada tredecim* belongs
to one of the four periodical cicadas
that emerges on a 13-year cycle.
Northern species of this genus have
a 17-year cycle. The mass emergence
of a particular species of periodical
cicadas in a particular U.S. region is
known as a "brood." Twenty-three
such broods have been identified
in the United States. The cicada
illustrated here is from brood XIX,
which occurs generally in the south-
central states, including southern
Illinois.

5 **Kissing bug, or cone-nose bug.**
Order Hemiptera, family Reduviidae,
Triatoma sanguisuga (LeConte)

Although commonly called "kissing
bugs," these bugs feed on the blood
of warm-blooded animals such as
rodents and raccoons. Often found in
tight-fitting crevices near their hosts,
these bugs normally live in wild areas
and rarely come into human habitations. Several species of *Triatoma* in
Latin America have caused enormous
human suffering because they act
as carriers of Chagas' disease (American trypanosomiasis). Research has
shown that *Triatoma* may sometimes
carry the pathogen in the United
States, but the incidence of that
is quite rare.

6 **Box elder bug.**
Order Hemiptera, family Rhopalidae,
Boisea trivittata (Say)

Rhopalid bugs lack scent glands and
most tend to feed on herbaceous
undergrowth. An exception is the
box elder bug, which feeds on box
elder (a kind of maple) and silver
maple trees. Adults overwinter and
breed in the spring. By fall they often

mass into spectacular populations
numbering in the thousands. Surprisingly, little damage is suffered by the
trees they feed on. The real nuisance
of this rhopalid occurs when they
enter houses in search of small
crevices in which to overwinter. On
warmer days in the winter, they may
emerge temporarily by the thousands
and bask in the sunlight on the
brighter, southern exposures of
homes. Although they are not harm-
ful to pets or people, homeowners
have noticed that they can leave
stains on curtains.

7 **Bark assassin bug.**
Order Hemiptera, family Reduviidae,
Microtomus purcis (Drury)

Bark assassin bugs can be found, as
their common name implies, under
bark where they feed on numerous
insect prey such as crickets, roaches,
and beetles.

PLATE X

Leafhoppers and Treehoppers

The former Homoptera is now included within the Hemiptera, though they lack the hard areas on the first pair of wings. These have the reputation of being the most destructive insects of all. They include aphids, leafhoppers, cicadas, and scale insects.

Like most other sap-feeding homopterans, leafhoppers feed on a liquid diet of extremely diluted sugar water. Relatively large quantities of plant sap must be ingested and processed for the leafhopper to benefit from the sugars, amino acids, and other nutrients that are present in such low quantities. Insects with such a feeding strategy are equipped with a highly modified gut that actually sends most of the ingested water directly to the hindgut, while special filters help retain important nutrients.

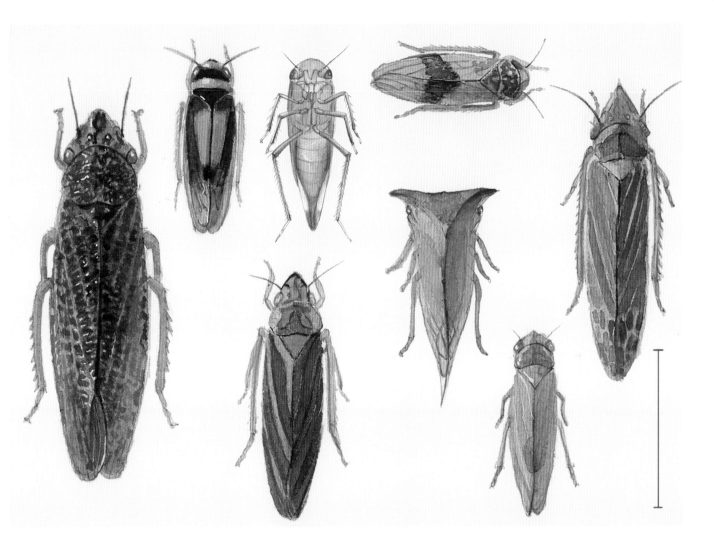

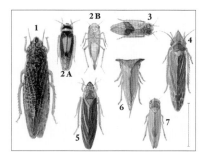

Excess sugars also bypass the midgut and are excreted as droplets called "honeydew," which is often sought by flies, ants, and other insects.

The membracids (treehoppers) are a family of insects that make an unusual living in the plantscape. Most live as mimics of thorns and processes that extend from plant stems. Some of the most bizarre insects are treehoppers. As xylem feeders, they are implicated as vectors of xylem-associated pathogens.

1 Sharpshooter.
Order Hemiptera, family Cicadellidae, *Graphocephala coccinea* (Forster)

The majority of leafhoppers are in one of two categories of sap feeders—xylem feeders or phloem feeders. Xylem tubes are canals in plants that move water from the roots to the rest of the plant. Phloem tubes are canals that transport carbohydrates from the leaves toward the roots. *Graphocephala coccinea* is a xylem feeder. It has a bulbous face that accommodates powerful sucking muscles, a typical feature of most xylem-feeding insects needed to overcome the negative pressure inside xylem tubes. This common garden species is among the more brightly colored of our leafhopper fauna.

2 Sharpshooter.
Order Hemiptera, family Cicadellidae, *Norvellina seminuda* (Say)

Many species of sharpshooters are known to cover their skin with a dust-like material called *brochosomes*. The origin of this material is an organ called the *Malphigian tubules*, which draw unwanted compounds from the blood and convert them into excretory products. Fluids from the hindgut, rich in brochosomes, are spread over the body and then dry into a fine white powder. This powdery layer is highly water resistant; a leading explanation for the function of brochosomes is that they repel honeydew from sticking to the leafhopper's skin. *Norvellina seminuda* is a phloem feeder and produces a rich honeydew. Figure 2A shows the upperside, 2B the underside.

3 Sharpshooter.
Order Hemiptera, family Cicadellidae, *Colladonus clitellarius* (Say)

A mysterious disease of stone-fruited trees of the genus *Prunus* was identified in 1933. Termed the *X-disease*, the causal agent has yet to be cultured in the laboratory. Now referred to as *phytoplasmas*, they have finally been classified as pathogenic phytobacteria without cell walls. These peculiar bacteria are known only to grow in the phloem tubes of various species of *Prunus*, and chokecherry seems to be the main reservoir in the United States. Phloem-feeding leafhoppers such as *C. clitellarius* and *N. seminuda* (figure 2) have been observed to be vectors of X-disease in the United States.

4 Potato leafhopper.
Order Hemiptera, family Cicadellidae, *Empoasca fabae* (Harris)

Leafhoppers belong to the family of bugs called *Cicadellidae*. Many species, such as *E. fabae*, cause commercial damage to crops. High densities of these leafhoppers may cause hopperburn in crops like sugar beet. Hopperburn is a moribund condition caused by exposure of the plant to the leafhopper's digestive fluids. The genus *Empoasca* contains many species that are quite difficult to identify because of their morphological resemblance to each other. Specialists must usually resort to microdissections to tell them apart.

5 Sharpshooter.
Order Hemiptera, family Cicadellidae, *Aulacizes irrorata* (Fabricius)

Aulacizes irrorata is another xylem-feeding leafhopper, like *Graphocephala coccinea*. These xylem feeders transmit the bacterium *Xylella fastidiosa* to many types of trees. This bacterium only lives in xylem tubes and is the cause of bacterial leaf scorch in many ornamental trees. The moribund disease is caused when bacterial proliferation actually causes plugs in the xylem canals and blocks the flow of water to the plant.

6 Buffalo treehopper.
Order Hemiptera, family Membracidae, *Ceresa bubalus* Fabricius

The buffalo treehopper, named for the appearance of its profile, passes through the winter as an egg, which is laid into slits made in twigs by the female. In spring, the newly emerged nymphs move to weedy open areas where they mature and find a mate. Recent studies in the behavior of treehoppers reveal that they locate each other by drumming messages. An amorous male vibrates his abdomen and the sound is transmitted throughout the plant. If a female is interested, she drums back a response, and the two eventually find each other. If the male hears no response, he tries his luck on another plant. Unfortunately, their conversations are not audible to human ears without the aid of audio equipment.

7 Sharpshooter.
Order Hemiptera, family Cicadellidae, *Draeculacephala noveboracensis* Fitch

There are many species of *Draeculacephala* in the United States. *Draeculacephala noveboracensis* is a very common transcontinental species, readily attracted to lights.

PLATE XI

Cicada

Dog-day cicada.
Order Hemiptera, family Cicadidae,
Tibicen dorsata (Say)

The dog-day cicada is the largest, bulkiest, and noisiest of all Illinois cicadas. Most people have heard the loud song produced in the late days of summer by this cicada. Life cycles of the dog-day cicada are not well known but life cycles of four to seven years have been recorded. Broods overlap for this species so that some of the adults appear each year. More well known are the periodical cicadas with their 13- and 17-year cycles and their synchronous emergence by the millions. The less known and much smaller prairie cicadas spend three to five years as nymphs feeding on the roots of prairie plants, especially prairie dock, whose flower stem is 8 feet tall. Adults emerge midsummer and can be fairly abundant in undisturbed prairies.

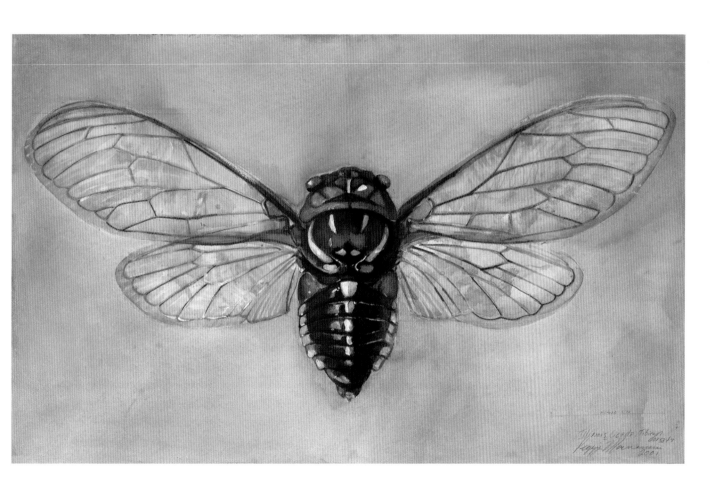

PLATE XII

Lacewings, Dobsonflies, and Their Kin

The order Neuroptera includes the lacewings and antlions (suborder Planipennia), dobsonflies and alderflies (suborder Megaloptera), and snakeflies (suborder Raphidoidea). Some classifications assign each of these groups to a separate order (Neuroptera, Megaloptera, and Raphidioptera, respectively) based on differences in structure and development.

Neuropterans are soft-bodied insects of variable size usually with longish antennae. They have biting and chewing mouthparts as both larvae and adults, although some of the adults do not feed. They generally have two pairs of wings, of which the hind pair are usually larger to some extent. The wings are normally held tent-like over their abdomen when not in flight, and many of the adults are relatively weak flyers. Those adults that feed do so on dead insects, nectar, and other liquids. The larvae are all carnivorous.

"Neuroptera"
Roger Swainston
2001

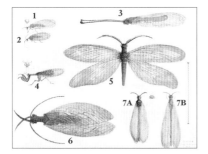

1 **Green lacewing.**
Order Neuroptera, family Chrysopidae, *Chrysoperla carnea* (Stephens)

The green lacewings comprise a small family of predaceous insects characterized by a network of lacelike veins supporting broad wings. The active larvae feed on most soft-bodied insects such as aphids or caterpillars, stabbing their prey with saber-like jaws and drawing in the body fluids. Adults attack similar kinds of prey and are capable of emitting a noxious odor when disturbed. Lacewing larvae can be cannibalistic. It is believed that chyrsopids developed a special adaptation in the egg to prevent cannibalism among their young: the female places each egg at the end of a long silken stalk, which the newly hatched larva must crawl down, thus never coming in contact with other eggs from its clutch.

2 **Brown lacewing.**
Order Neuroptera, family Hemerobiidae, *Hemerobius stigmaterus* (Fitch)

Brown lacewings—brown in color and smaller in size—are a family separate from chrysopids. Although similar in habit to the green lacewings, the larvae of brown lacewings conceal themselves by attaching bits of debris found in their habitats to their thorny backs. Also unlike green lacewings, hermerobiids do not attach eggs to silken stalks; instead they glue eggs singly or in groups to apple buds or twigs where there are aphid colonies. Larvae eat more than 20 aphids per day.

3 **Owlfly.**
Order Neuroptera, family Ascalaphidae, *Ululodes quadrimaculatus* (Say)

Owlflies look like dragonflies but they can be easily distinguished by their long, clubbed antennae. They are nocturnal and usually rest during the day against a twig with their abdomen bent upward at a ninety-degree angle to the rest of their body. They fly at dusk, preying on smaller insects. Their young can be found stalking other insects in ground litter.

4 Mantisfly.
Order Neuroptera, family Mantispidae, *Mantispa sayi* (Banks)

Members of this small family resemble tiny praying mantids and share the voracious reputation of their namesakes. Equally unusual are the habits of the immature stages of *Mantispa*. All are known predators of spider eggs. As a young larva, an *M. sayi* boards a passing spider, then penetrates the spider's egg sac while it is being constructed. As is true of all neuropteran larvae, the mandibles of mantispid larvae have a hollow channel that runs down the length of the mandible. Once pierced by the mandibles, the egg's fluids are sucked into the mouth through this channel.

5 Fishfly.
Order Megaloptera, family Corydalidae, *Chauliodes rastricornis* (Rambur)

Chauliodes is a smaller relative of the dobsonfly (figure 6) but has serrated antennae and grayish wings. Like dobsonflies, fishfly larvae are predaceous on other aquatic insects and hunt by holding onto the streambed with two hooks at the end of their abdomen while using their forebody to wrestle with prey. Larvae leave the water to pupate beneath objects near the stream.

6 Dobsonfly.
Order Megaloptera, family Corydalidae, *Corydalus cornutus* (Linnaeus)

These insects are some of the largest of the Illinois fauna, reaching lengths of more than 50 mm. Their aquatic larvae, called *hellgrammites*, are prized bait for people fishing for smallmouth bass and brook trout. The males are unusual—their two mandibles are prolonged and tusklike but, despite the alarming appearance, are weak and incapable of inflicting harm. Many species of the Corydalidae are attracted to lights; homeowners who live near rivers can expect dobsonflies to swirl around their porch lights.

7 Antlions.
Order Neuroptera, family Myrmeleontidae, *Myrmeleon immaculatus* (DeGeer) and *Cryptoleon signatum* (Hagen)

Antlions are renowned for the habits of their larvae (also known as "doodlebugs"), which excavate a funnel-shaped pit in sandy soil by walking in a spiral and flicking sand out of the funnel with their heads. When finished, they bury themselves at the bottom of the pit, their large, falcate mandibles cocked in an open position. The construction of these sand pits is intentional; insect prey that stumble into an antlion pit slip and slide down the slope (just as anyone who has climbed a sand dune experiences the inherent tendency to slide down with each upward step).

Antlions hasten the process by flicking sand on the escaping victim. Once at the bottom there is little chance of escape for the prey. Antlions are not immune to enemies, however. Females of a chalcid wasp, *Lasiochalcidia igilienis* (Masi), provoke antlions to attack. Although the wasp allows herself to be captured, she is armed with a pair of enlarged hind legs, which she uses to hold the antlion's jaws open. While the antlion struggles with the wasp, the wasp injects an egg into the antlion's soft neck where it grows into an internal parasite and eventually kills its host. The wasp escapes to lay her eggs in other victims. Figure 7A is *Myrmeleon immaculatus* (DeGeer), 7B is *Cryptoleon signatum* (Hagen).

PLATE XIII

Flies

"Flies," "mosquitoes," "gnats," "midges," and "no-see-ums" are common names for different members of the order Diptera. Dipterans typically have sucking mouthparts, and may feed on plant juices or decaying organic matter. A number of dipterans feed on blood, and some may transmit diseases; certain mosquitoes transmit malaria.

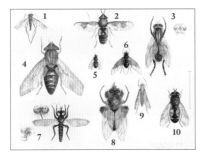

1 Long-legged fly.
Order Diptera, family
Dolichopodidae (unidentified species)

These small- to medium-sized flies
are usually shiny green metallic
and are predators of other insects.
Dolichopodids are common and can
be found in many different habitats,
especially meadows and marshy
areas.

2 Deer fly.
Order Diptera, family Tabanidae,
Chrysops excitans (Walker)

Smaller cousins of horse flies, deer
flies have similar habits and developmental stages. They are particularly
bothersome to hikers in shaded
woods and readily swarm around
one's hair in great numbers. Many
species occur in Illinois, including
C. excitans, whose Latin name con-
notes a rude "awakening" when it
bites. Larvae of deer flies differ from
those of horse flies in that they are
detritivores (i.e., they feed on detri-
tus, or loose decaying material).

Unlike the mouthparts of mosquitoes, tabanid mouthparts are not
adapted for piercing skin. Instead
females cut the skin surface with tiny
sharp blades, then lap up the pooling
blood. Blood-feeding insects, including tabanids, have the potential for
transmitting diseases to humans and
animals. Some *Chrysops* species serve
as vectors of diseases in humans. The
ocular worm parasite *Loa loa* is transmitted by deerflies in Africa. Tu-
laremia, a bacterial disease, has been
transmitted to humans occasionally
in the United States by *Chrysops
discalis* Williston.

3 Flesh fly.
Order Diptera, family Sarcophagidae,
Sarcophaga bullata (Parker)

Adult flesh flies are found on flowers
and carrion. Unlike blow flies, which
lay eggs, female flesh flies deposit
living larvae on the remains of animals—an adaptation, perhaps, for
the rapid colonization of food
sources, since the eggs of competing
flies require an incubation period.
The larvae, called "maggots," can
rapidly dispose of even large carcasses and, for this reason, play an
important role in community ecol-
ogy. This is a very diverse genus, with
many species in Illinois.

4 Green-headed horse fly.
Order Diptera, family Tabanidae,
Tabanus americanus Forester

Moderate to large biting flies, the
numerous species of horse flies in
Illinois are found in wooded and
wood-edge habitats near water. The
brilliant green head of *T. americanus* is
actually a reflection from their eyes
that quickly fades in preserved specimens. Both sexes feed on flower
nectar and pollen, but eventually

females require blood meals to produce eggs. Eggs are laid on plant surfaces near water. The aquatic larvae are voracious predators of other invertebrates. They overwinter in the water and emerge as adults later in the spring.

Like *Chrysops*, species of *Tabanus* can also serve as vectors of disease in humans. Although this is more prevalent in tropical countries, members of the genus *Tabanus* have been know to transmit California encephalitis to domesticated animals in the United States.

5 **Blow fly.**

Order Diptera, family Calliphoridae, greenbottle fly *Phaenicia sericata* (Meigen)

Often shiny green, blue, or black, calliphorid flies, known as "blow flies," an English term referring to their egg-laying habits, are similar in habitats and development to flesh flies. This species, as well as other calliphorid and sarcophagid flies, is often the first wave of the succession of insects that attack cadavers. The field of forensic entomology often employs the knowledge

of life cycles to help investigators determine how long human cadavers have been dead.

6 **Bee fly.**

Order Diptera, family Bombyliidae, *Anthrax analis* (Say)

Ornamented with tufts of scales and hairs that give them the appearance of bees, the bombyliids are found around flowers or searching near ground vegetation for hosts on which to lay their eggs. This entire group of flies is presumed to be parasitic on other insects, such as beetles, butterflies, bees, and other flies. *Anthrax analis* is a parasitoid of tiger beetle larvae. Female flies locate the tunnel of a larval tiger beetle, wait until the owner retreats to the bottom of its burrow, and then deposit one to several eggs at the entrance, which fall to the bottom of the tunnel. The hatched larva temporarily attaches to its host, living as an external parasite on the beetle larva. Only when the tiger beetle larva grows large enough does the larva of *A. analis* consume and kill it. The mature larva then pupates and emerges as an adult fly.

7 **Robber fly.**

Order Diptera, family Asilidae (unidentfied species)

Named for their predatory habits on other insects, robber flies can often be seen waiting on perches in open areas to ambush other insects that happen to fly too close. Their larvae live in the soil or in decayed wood where they seem to be predators of other insects.

8 **Robber fly.**

Order Diptera, family Asilidae, *Laphria sicula* (McAtee)

The genus *Laphria* contains many species that resemble wasps and bees. *Laphria sicula* has the shape and steel-blue color of many kinds of solitary wasps. Because birds and lizards that feed on insects learn to associate the sting of bumble bees with their bright yellow markings, nonstinging flies, such as *L. sacrator*, benefit by wearing the same colors.

9 **Wood fly.**

Order Diptera, family Xylophagidae, *Dialysis rufithorax* (Say)

Xylophagids are a small family of primitive flies. The adults are usually found in moist woods, especially near water. Adult xylophagids take in fluids from plant sources. The larvae live in moist decaying wood. Little is known about the habits of *D. rufithorax*; presumably the larvae are predators on smaller insects that occur beneath the bark and cavities of decaying wood.

10 **Hover fly.**

Order Diptera, family Syrphidae, *Baccha elongata* (Fabricus)

Usually brightly marked, hover flies often mimic bees and wasps. They can often be seen near flowers but are avoided by predators because of their deceptive colors. The larvae of many species, including those of *Baccha*, are predators of aphids and psyllids. The whitish larvae ply up and down stems waving the front part of their bodies back and forth until they encounter their prey.

PLATE XIV

Moths I

Moths and butterflies belong to the order Lepidoptera. The majority of Lepidoptera are moths. Most adult butterflies are active during the day and brightly colored. Their bodies are generally slender and not especially hairy. Adult moths are generally active at night or at dawn or dusk. Most moths are drab, with cryptic wing patterns. Their bodies tend to be bulky and are often quite hairy.

The shape of the antennae is the best way to distinguish butterflies from moths. Except for one group of tropical butterflies, all butterflies have simple antennae that end in a swelling, or "club." Moth antennae range in shape from simple to feather-like, but all of them lack the clubbed tip. There are no simple characteristics that universally distinguish moth caterpillars or pupae from those of butterflies.

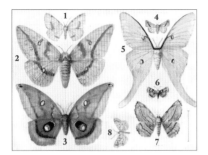

1 **False crocus geometer moth.**
Order Lepidoptera, family Geometridae, *Xanthotype urticaria* (Swett)

This moth belongs to a family well
known for its highly characteristic
caterpillars, the inchworms. The
moth feeds on a variety of foods,
including catnip, ivy, and goldenrods.
Because its food source is commonly
available, the moth is widespread and
often found locally in large numbers.

2 **Imperial moth.**
Order Lepidoptera, family
Saturniidae, *Eacles imperialis* (Drury)

This large yellow moth is very im-
pressive. Like most saturniids, it does
not feed as an adult; the moth lives
its entire life off the copious amounts
of food it consumed as a caterpillar.
This species is known for its very
large, fierce-looking caterpillar (75- to
100-mm long). The four spines on its
head and bright yellow spots running
along its body are presumably deter-
rents to predators. The caterpillars
feed on conifers, birches, oaks, etc.,
depending on the region.

3 **Polyphemus moth.**
Order Lepidoptera, family Saturniidae, *Antheraea polyphemus* (Cramer)

This very popular moth is well
known for the two large eyespots on
its hind wings, which are believed to
be a deterrent to predators. When
disturbed, the moth raises its
forewings and flashes the eyespots,
frightening the predator away. They
are primarily oak feeders and have
huge, green caterpillars.

4 **Clouded crimson moth.**
Order Lepidoptera, family Noctuidae,
Schinia gaurae (Smith)

Moths in the genus *Schinia* are
known for their close affiliation with
prairies. They often feed on rare or
highly specific plants found in pris-
tine or restored prairies. The clouded
crimson moth feeds on the biennial
gaure plant. These moths are highly
sensitive to environmental change
and can be indicators of the health
of the prairie system.

5 **Luna moth.**
Order Lepidoptera, family
Saturniidae, *Actias luna* (Linnaeus)

The luna moth is undoubtedly the
most commonly known and loved
moth species. The brilliant lime-
green coloration and long tails act
as camouflage and a defense system.
The expendable tail is used to draw
the attention of an attacking predator away from the moth's body.

6 **Leadplant flower moth.**
Order Lepidoptera, family Noctuidae,
Schinia lucens (Morrison)

This beautiful moth is a rare occurrence among prairie moths. It is an
excellent indicator of the health of a
prairie system. It feeds on the flowers
and seeds of the leadplant flower.

7 **Common lytrosis.**
Order Lepidoptera, family
Geometridae, *Lytrosis unitaria*
(Herrich-Schäffer)

This common lytrosis is a large
geometrid, or inchworm moth. The
caterpillar is known as a twig mimic;
it appears as if it is a twig, hanging
off a branch. It feeds mainly on
hawthorns, pin oak, and sugar
maple trees.

8 **Ironweed pyralid.**
Order Lepidoptera, family Pyralidae,
Polygrammodes flavidalis (Guenée)

This moth is common in prairies
where there is a high occurrence of
ironweed. The irregular patterns on
the wings break up the outline of the
moth and confuse predators. This
moth's caterpillar bores into the
roots of ironweed.

PLATE XV   *Moths II*

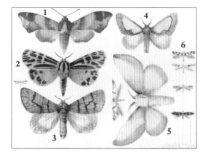

1 Hog sphinx moth, or Virginia creeper sphinx.
Order Lepidoptera, family Sphingidae, *Darapsa myron* (Cramer)

Good fliers with a very rapid wing beat, the hog sphinx adults are medium- to large-sized moths with thick antennae. Note the thick, wide bodies and relatively narrow wings. The caterpillar has jowl-like body segments behind the head and feeds on Virginia creeper and grape leaves. Although the caterpillars may cause damage, they can be picked off easily by hand and they have a natural enemy in the parasitic wasps of the family Ichneumonidae.

2 Oithona tiger moth.
Order Lepidoptera, family Arctidae, *Grammia oithona* (Strecker)

These beautifully colored tiger moths are spotted, banded, or both. While the species is still common in the Midwest, its range has been threatened in the Northeast. Fewer and fewer of these pretty moths are seen around cities and suburbs, where development of new housing, industry, and high-tech agriculture have eaten away at their wide habitats.

3 Eastern panthea.
Order Lepidoptera, family Noctuidae, *Panthea furcilla* (Packard)

The Noctuidae, or owlet family, is the largest family of moths with some 20,000 species worldwide. There are about 2,900 North American species that run the gamut from downright drab to outrageously gaudy. This moth feeds on conifers; spruce, pines, and tamaracks are its preferred diet.

4 **Spiny oak slug moth.**
Order Lepidoptera, family Limacodidae, *Euclea delphinii* (Boisduval)

These moths have broad bodies and rounded wings. Although the Illinois fauna includes a number of species, *Euclea* are found more broadly in the tropics. The larvae, commonly known as "slug caterpillars," feed on beeches, chestnuts, and maples.

5 **Rosy maple moth.**
Order Lepidoptera. Family Saturniidae, *Dryocampa rubicunda* (Fabricius)

One of the silkworm moths, the rosy maple moth lives up to its name: a rosy pink color forms the border of its wings and fills up all but the median areas. The caterpillar is known as the "green-striped mapleworm" and feeds predominantly on silver maples and also on oaks.

6 **Microlepidoptera.**
Several different families of "micro-moth" lepidoptera

The size of these tiny moths varies, but they typically have a wingspan of 20 mm or less. When magnified (these were painted by looking through a microscope), the "micros" show as much beauty and diversity of form and style as do the giants. Special techniques must be learned to collect, prepare, and study these little gems, which often make up about 50 percent of the fauna in any given area. Many are leaf miners: the larvae leave characteristic "mines" (tiny etched lines) in the leaves they feed on.

PLATE XVI

Common Butterflies

All of the butterflies on this plate occur in the Illinois region to a greater or lesser extent, depending on habitat, host plants, climatic factors, time of year, and periodic fluctuations in population dynamics. Keen observers can find them all if they know where and when to look for them!

1 Mourning cloak.
Order Lepidoptera, family Nymphalidae, *Nymphalis antiopa* (Linnaeus)

A large, rich-brown butterfly with a ragged border, this is often the first butterfly seen during the year. It overwinters as an adult, and can be seen on warm days as early as January. It prefers open woods, watercourses and their borders, as well as landscaped areas.

2 Cabbage white.
Order Lepidoptera, family Pieridae, *Pieris rapae* (Linnaeus)

Considered a weed species because of its ubiquitous presence, the cabbage white butterfly was introduced "accidentally" in Canada in 1860 from Europe. It can be found virtually everywhere, except in the most extreme environmental conditions. The caterpillar feeds on cabbage and other mustards, and is considered an agricultural pest.

3 Red admiral.
Order Lepidoptera, family Nymphalidae, *Vanessa atalanta* (Linnaeus)

This highly erratic, territorial species migrates north from the Southwest every year in the spring to repopulate. The caterpillar feeds on nettle (*Urtica*) and false nettle (*Boehmeria*). The adult butterfly can be found in urban as well as rural environments.

4 Orange sulphur.
Order Lepidoptera, family Pieridae, *Colias eurytheme* (Boisduval)

A common butterfly found in a variety of habitats, both urban and rural. The caterpillar feeds on plants in the pea family, including alfalfa and white clover. Adults gather nectar from a variety of plants, mostly members of the daisy family.

5 Painted lady.
Order Lepidoptera, family Nymphalidae, *Vanessa cardui* (Linnaeus)

A flighty, widely distributed butterfly, the painted lady is most often seen nectaring, especially on thistle in open areas. Large populations of this species are periodic, depending on climatic conditions in the Southwest from which it migrates. This species is frequently reared and released by school children.

6 Milbert's tortoiseshell.
Order Lepidoptera, family Nymphalidae, *Nymphalis milberti* (Godart)

Milbert's tortoiseshell is a dark orange and brown, irregular-bordered butterfly that prefers northern climes. Its caterpillar feeds on nettle (*Urtica*), but the adult butterfly can be found in almost any habitat where cool weather prevails.

7 Comma.
Order Lepidoptera, family Nymphalidae, *Polygonia comma* (Harris)

The comma is an anglewing butterfly found near open woods and watercourses. It gets its name from the tiny comma-shaped metallic marking on the underside of the lower wing. Commas are fast and erratic flyers, but when perched, they resemble dead leaves and blend in with their wooded surroundings.

8 Buckeye.
Order Lepidoptera, family Nymphalidae, *Junonia coenia* (Hübner)

This small, brightly patterned butterfly is found in open fields, roadsides, railroad grades, and other open edges. A hot-weather butterfly of low cold tolerance, its late summer brood migrates south from its northern climes.

9 Monarch.
Order Lepidoptera, family Nymphalidae, *Danaus plexippus* (Linnaeus)

Our most well-known butterfly, its bold orange and black markings, large size, and mass southerly fall migration are its identifying characteristics. Called the "milkweed butterfly," its caterpillar feeds on *Asclepias* plants and is often toxic as a result. Adults overwinter in remote mountain colonies in Mexico. It is Illinois' only true northward and southward migratory species and is the state butterfly.

10 Summer azure.
Order Lepidoptera, family Lycaenidae, *Celastrina neglecta* (Edwards)

This tiny "blue" can generally be found along woodland edges. Often mistaken for eastern tailed blues from a distance, it is easily identified by its high spiral flight as opposed to the characteristic low flight of the eastern tailed blue. Summer azures are lighter and less mottled than their spring counterparts and more widely distributed in their habitat preferences.

11 American copper.
Order Lepidoptera, family Lycaenidae, *Lycaena phlaeas americana* (Harris)

This tiny, purple and coppery-orange butterfly is found in open, sunny, disturbed areas and flies relatively low to the ground. Males are territorial and maintain preferred perches. There is debate about the origin of this butterfly.

12 White admiral.
Order Lepidoptera, family Nymphalidae, *Basilarchia arthemis* (Drury)

The white admiral is a relatively uncommon northern Illinois species that intergrades with the red-spotted purple (*Limenitis arthemis astyanax*) (figure 13) in northern parts of its range. A forest dweller, it is sometimes found in urban areas if its larval host trees (such as birch, willow, and poplar) are present. Its behavior is similar to the red-spotted purple.

13 Red-spotted purple.
Order Lepidoptera, family Nymphalidae, *Basilarchia arthemis astyanax* (Fabricius)

This attractive mimic of the toxic pipevine swallowtail (*Battus philenor*) is generally found near open woodlands and forest edges. In northern parts of its range, it is known to hybridize with the white admiral (*Limenitis arthemis arthemis*), another subspecies of the species. Adults feed on sap, rotting fruit, carrion, and animal dung.

14 Northern pearly eye.
Order Lepidoptera, family Nymphalidae, *Enodia anthedon* Clark

The northern pearly eye is a deciduous woodland butterfly found in clearings and edges. Adults feed on willow and birch sap, and perch on trees or shrubs. A highly mobile butterfly, it is often hard to identify. The caterpillar feeds on woodland grasses and the adult is unusually shade tolerant.

PLATE XVII

Swallowtails

These large, showy, prominently tailed butterflies in the family Papilion-idae have all three pairs of legs fully developed for walking and perching. The larvae have a retractable gland, called an *osmeterium*, which emits a foul odor when the caterpillar is disturbed. The adult males of this family are known to congregate at mud holes to absorb salts and minerals from the soil to enhance their "virility."

1 **Pipevine swallowtail.**
Order Lepidoptera, family Papilionidae, *Battus philenor* (Linnaeus)

This beautiful metallic blue-black butterfly has many mimics because of its bad taste to predators. The caterpillar feeds mainly on pipevine plants, which makes the adult distasteful. The caterpillars vary from black with red-orange spikes all along their bodies to all red-orange.

2 **Giant swallowtail.**
Order Lepidoptera, family Papilionidae, *Papilio cresphontes* Cramer

Our largest butterfly, it is distinctive for its size and broad horizontal yellow band across the dorsal forewings. More common in the southern part of its range, the larvae feed on citrus and ash trees. The mature caterpillar is brown or olive and resembles a large bird dropping. A strong flyer and glider, the adult can travel long distances and is found in open areas along rivers, woodland edges, glades, and citrus groves, where it is sometimes considered a pest.

3 **Black swallowtail.**
Order Lepidoptera, family Papilionidae, *Papilio polyxenes asterius* Stoll

A common swallowtail found in parks, gardens, meadows, roadsides, and other open areas, both urban and suburban. Males search for high spots in vegetation to patrol and wait for females. The caterpillars feed mainly on plants in the carrot family, such as dill and Queen Anne's lace. The mature larva is bright green with black bands containing yellow spots on each segment.

4 **Spicebush swallowtail.**
Order Lepidoptera, family Papilion-
idae, *Papilio troilus* Linnaeus

The spicebush swallowtail butterfly
is a large, dark swallowtail. It is one
of our most beautiful and interesting
swallowtails. The larvae feed on
spicebush, sassafras trees, perhaps
prickly ash, tulip tree, sweetbay,
camphor, and redbay. The caterpillars
make nests of the leaves by spinning
silk and curling the leaf up, then hide
in the nest in the daytime and come
out at night to eat. Young caterpillars
are small and brown-green in color.
Older caterpillars are bright green
with large primary eyespots and
resemble a small snake, possibly
to warn off predators.

5 **Zebra swallowtail.**
Order Lepidoptera, family Papilion-
idae, *Eurytides marcellus* (Cramer)

This zebra-striped, triangular-winged
butterfly with long, sharp tails lays its
eggs on pawpaw (*Asimina triloba*). A
fast flyer, it darts from plant to plant
while nectaring. It prefers lakes, wet
woodlands near rivers, and open
brushland and rarely strays far from

its source of pawpaw. Young larvae
are dark colored with many trans-
verse black, yellow, and white bands,
while the older larvae are green with
broad blue, black, and yellow trans-
verse bands between the thorax and
abdomen.

6 **Eastern tiger swallowtail.**
Order Lepidoptera, family Papilion-
idae, *Papilio glaucus* Linnaeus

Probably the most popular swallowtail, this butterfly is found in hardwoods, forest edges, river valleys,
parks, and suburbs. The males are
yellow with black tiger stripes. Some
female swallowtails have the same
color pattern as the males, some are
completely black, while others are a
variation in between. The larvae feed
on leaves of various plants, including
wild cherry, sweetbay, basswood,
tulip tree, birch, ash, cottonwood,
mountain ash, and willow. The young
larvae are dark and resemble bird
droppings, while older larvae are
smooth green with a single pair of
yellow and blue false eyespots on
the third segment of the thorax.

PLATE XVIII

Beetles

Beetles are in the order Coleoptera, which is the largest order in the animal kingdom. In the United States and Canada, there are about 25,000 species. The beetle families with the most North American species are the rove beetles (Staphylinidae, 4,100 species), the weevils (Curculionidae, about 2,400 species), the ground beetles (Carabidae, 1,700 species), the leaf beetles (Chrysomelidae, about 1,700 species), the scarab beetles (Scarabaeidae, about 1,500 species), the darkling beetles (Tenebrionidae, 1,200 species), and the long-horned beetles (Cerambycidae, about 1,000 species).

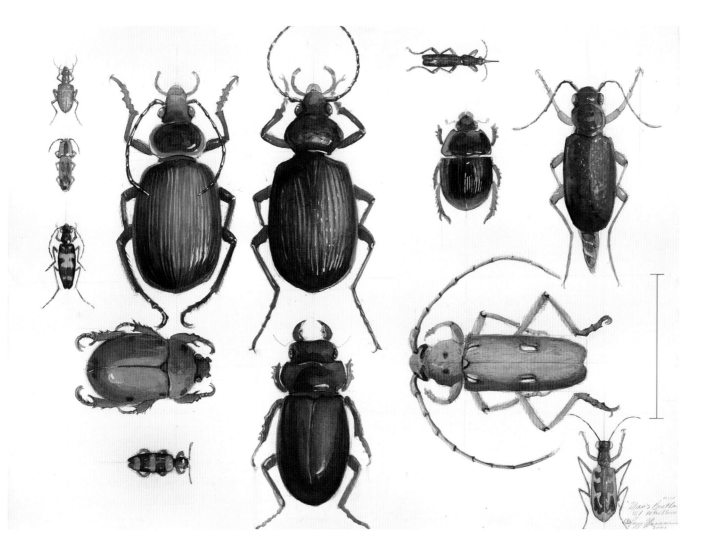

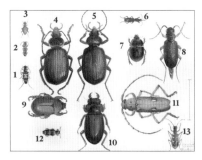

1 **Long-horned beetle.**
Order Coleoptera, family Cerambycidae, *Typocerus sparsus* (LeConte)

Cerambycid beetles, which include
some of the largest beetles in the
world, are characterized by their
elongated antennae and often brightly
colored patterns. These features make
this family particularly attractive to
amateur collectors. Children are often
fascinated by captive adults, which
emit a raspy sound by stridulating.
Adult females lay their eggs on trees
and shrubs, or the stems of herbs.
Some species take up to several years
to mature. Adults of *T. sparsus* fly from
June through August and are often
found taking nectar from flowers.
The larvae feed on dead pine trees.

2 **Click beetle.**
Order Coleoptera, family Elateridae,
Aeolus mellillus (Say)

Elaterids are known as the "click
beetles." This epithet derives from
their ability to right themselves by
snapping two body parts together, an
action that hurls them into the air
like acrobats. Their larvae, commonly referred to as "wireworms,"
live in the soil where they attack the
roots of plants. *Aeolus mellilus* (5–7.5
mm) is a common beetle found in
lawns, vegetation, and flowers, and
is sometimes attracted to lights.

3 **False tiger beetle.**
See plate XIX, figure 7

4 **Fiery searcher, or
caterpillar hunter.**
Order Coleoptera, family Carabidae,
Calosoma scrutator (Fabricius)

Ground beetles, or Carabidae,
comprise one of the largest families
of beetles. Most live as predators on
other insects; a few have switched to
seed predation and some have even
become parasitic. *Calosoma scrutator*
(25–30 mm) lives in open wooded
areas and sometimes can be found
on shrubs in cities. It climbs trees for
its preferred prey—the caterpillars
of many forest moths and butterflies.
The caterpillar hunter is one of
Illinois' most handsome ground
beetles.

5 **Fiery hunter.**
Order Coleoptera, family Caribadae,
Calosoma calidum (Fabricius)

This big beetle preys on caterpillars.
Adults climb trees in search of prey
during the day. They overwinter in
soil or in sheltered sites and then
emerge in spring and lay eggs. Larvae
prey on soil-dwelling species and
then pupate in soil. Adults remain
in the soil until they emerge the
following spring.

6 **Oak timberworm, or
straight-snouted weevil.**
Order Coleoptera, family Brentidae,
Arrhenodes minutus (Drury)

The brentids are a group of weevil-
like beetles that contain, among their
various forms, some of the most
slender, elongated beetles on the
planet. The larvae feed in wood while
the adults can be found under bark or
in logs, where some are predators and
others feed on fungi or sap. Females
of *A. minutus* chew holes into the
bark of red or white oak in which
they lay their eggs. The larvae then
bore into the deeper layers of wood.

They require up to three years to mature into adults. This species is a commercial pest of the timber industry.

7 Dumbledor beetle.
Order Coleoptera, family Geotrupidae, *Geotrupes semiopacus* Jekel

These mostly bright, metallic-colored beetles (12–20 mm) provide their larvae with meals of dung or rotting vegetation. Adults often feed on dung or fungi, and most live in tunnels. They can often be found at lights. There are many instances where *Geotrupes* has become the focus of European folklore. The Greek playwright Menander, for example, uses *Geotrupes* as a steed to carry the hero Trygaios to Zeus.

8 Tiger beetle.
See plate XIX, figure 5

9 Grapevine beetle.
Order Coleoptera, family Scarabaeidae, *Pelidnota punctata* (Linnaeus)

Scarabaeidae comprise a large and diverse family of beetles, many of considerable economic importance because of the leaf-eating habits of many adults and root-feeding of many larvae. Some of the largest and most colorful beetles belong to this family. Scarabs are highly prized among amateur collectors. *Pelidnota punctata* (20–25 mm) feeds on grape foliage and fruits, and is often found near wooded areas.

10 "Pinching bug," or stag beetle.
Order Coleoptera, family Lucanidae, *Lucanus capreolus* (Linnaeus)

The lucanids, or stag beetles, are named for the resemblance of the jaws of some male stag beetles to the antlers of deer. Many species are dimorphic—the males show an exaggerated growth of the mandibles while the females (like this one) do not. The large *L. capreolus* (22–35 mm) usually attracts attention when adults emerge from rotten wood. Although

sluggish in their movements, they will stand their ground and bite any attacker, including the occasional curious child.

11 Ivory-marked long-horned beetle.
Order Coleoptera, family Cerambycidae, *Eburia quadrigeminata* (Say)

Spines decorate the legs and wingtips of this longhorn (14–24 mm). The larvae bore into dry maple, chestnut, oak, hickory, ash, and cypress. The adults, which are known to come to light, feed on foliage and twigs. Larvae trapped in finished wood have been known to emerge decades later.

12 Nutall's trichodes, or red-and-blue-checkered beetle.
Order Coleoptera, family Cleridae, *Trichodes nutalli* (Kirby)

Typically bright-colored, the clerid beetles are mostly predators. Found on trees and vegetation, adults of *T. nutalli* often come to flowers where they feed on pollen as well as small insects such as thrips. Their larvae wait in flowers and attach themselves

to visiting bees or wasps, thus allowing themselves to be carried to their host's nest where the beetle larvae parasitize and feed on the host's young.

13 Ghost tiger beetle.
Order Coleoptera, family Carabidae, *Cicindela lepida* Dejean

Ghost tiger beetles are typically 9–11 mm with a dorsal surface of white or cream. They have good eyesight to about 3–4 feet. When they fly from a predator, they can land facing it so they can see predators approach. The head and thorax are green or reddish and covered by white setae. Maculations are greatly expanded and leave only small areas of light brown. Habitats include pure white to pale yellow, dry, sandy areas with sparse or no vegetation, including coastal sand dunes and inland sand pits. They are usually found on coastal shorelines, or large lake shores, but can be found on sand flats away from water and on dunes well inland. This is a summer species with a 2-year life cycle.

PLATE XIX

Tiger Beetles and Look-alikes

Tiger beetles are a diverse group of ground beetles. Some beetle special-ists still consider them a separate family called the *Cicindelidae*. The com-mon name derives from their voracious and active predatory habits. Adult tiger beetles hunt by stealth and quickly pounce on their prey when close. The larvae dig burrows, usually in sandy soil, where they wait at the tops of their burrows to pounce on any insect that may happen to pass. Tiger beetles hold the land speed record among arthropods. When scaled to hu-man dimensions, the ambush of some species is equivalent to more than 300 miles per hour!

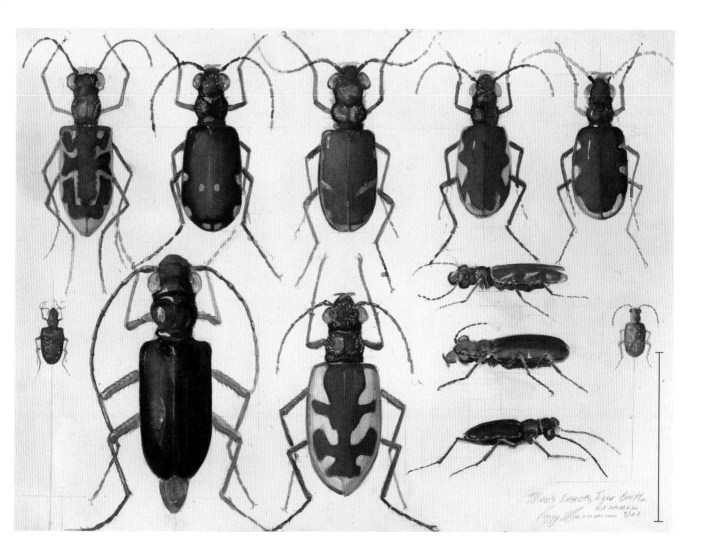

Illinois Insects, Tiger Beetle
10x actual size
Peggy Macnamara 9/01

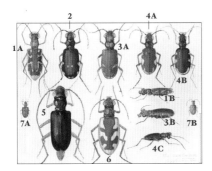

1 **Coppery tiger beetle.**
Order Coleoptera, family Carabidae,
Cicindela cuprescens (LeConte)

Cicindela cuprescens is commonly
found in sandy areas along rivers.
Figure 1A shows the top view, 1B
shows the side view.

2 **Six-spotted tiger beetle.**
Order Coleoptera, family Carabidae,
Cicindela sexguttata (Fabricius)

This species is the only Illinois
forest dweller and is the familiar
tiger beetle often seen along shaded
trails and paths in forest preserves.
Cicindela sexguttata is an unusual tiger
beetle in that the adults emerge
from their pupal stage in the fall,
but remain in their pupal chambers
until the following spring.

3 **Clay bank tiger beetle.**
Order Coleoptera, family Carabidae,
Cicindela limbalis (Klug)

The clay bank tiger beetle prefers
sloping soils with high clay content.
It is common on riverbanks, hillsides,
and roadcuts. Adults are seen in
spring and fall. Figure 3A shows the
top view, 3B shows the side view.

4 **Smooth tiger beetle.**
Order Coleoptera, family Carabidae,
Cicindela scutellaris lecontei
(Haldeman) and *Cicindela scutellaris
rugifrons* Dejean

The smooth tiger beetle is usually
red-purplish-bronze (figure 4A) with
smooth elytra but a green subspecies
is known, *C. scutellaris rugifrons* (figure
4B). This tiger beetle tolerates drier
habitats such as road cuts, sand
pits, or open sandy areas with sparse
vegetation. Often found with *C. formosa generosa* (see figure 6). Figure 4C
shows the side view.

5 **Virginia big-headed tiger beetle.**
Order Coleoptera, family Carabidae,
Megacephala virginica (Linnaeus)

This flightless tiger beetle is found
in southern Illinois where it inhabits
open areas. Adults are active hunters
from dusk to dawn but hide under
boards or rocks during the day. They
are often seen at streetlights where
they dine on other insects.

6 **Big sand tiger beetle.**
Order Coleoptera, family Carabidae,
Cicindela formosa generosa (Dejean)

This beetle is the largest *Cicindela*
in Illinois and is found in dry sandy
areas, stream banks, dry forest clearings, sand pits, and sand dune edges.
Often found with *C. scutellaris
lecontei* (see figure 5).

7 **False tiger beetle.**
Order Coleoptera, family Carabidae,
Elaphrus (unidentified species)

These beetles (figures 7A and 7B) have
much the same general shape as tiger
beetles but are not closely related to
them within the Carabidae. They are
predators that live along the muddy
banks of streams and lakes. At least
five species of *Elaphrus* occur in
Illinois.

PLATE XX

Rove Beetles and Carrion Beetles

This plate shows rove beetles (order Coleoptera, family Staphylinidae) and carrion beetles (order Coleoptera, family Silphidae). Species of both groups are more numerous in forests or woodlands than in open areas, although some species do prefer prairies, coastal dunes, or other more open places. Most rove beetles are predaceous, feeding on insects, nematodes, or other smaller invertebrates. Some, however, have evolved different habits and eat fungi, rotting wood, or leaves, or even pollen from flowers. Except for those feeding in flowers, rove beetles usually are hard to find because they spend their lives hidden in such places as leaf litter, soil, and logs. No one knows for sure, but Illinois probably has at least 500 resident species of rove beetles. Of the 4,100 species known to occur in

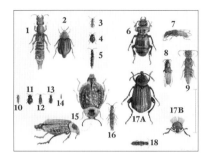

North America, over 300 have been collected in Cook and Will counties.

Carrion beetles, as their name suggests, are associated with decaying animal remains. Nearly all carrion beetle larvae feed only on carrion, but some adults also eat maggots, and adults and larvae of a few species (not occurring in Illinois) eat leaves of plants. See figures 2, 6, 15, and 17.

1 **Rove beetle.**
Order Coleoptera, family
Staphylinidae, *Platydracus maculosus*
(Gravenhorst)

This is the largest rove beetle species
in North America, reaching up to
about 1.2 inch (30 mm) long. Adults
are strongly attracted to carrion,
dung, and other decaying material,
where they feed on maggots or other
insects.

2 **Carrion beetle.**
Order Coleoptera, family Silphidae,
Oiceoptoma noveboracense (Forster)

This widespread species is active
and breeding in springtime, feeding
and breeding on carrion in forested
areas. Its pinkish pronotum (the
section behind the head) is very
distinctive; it is small for a carrion
beetle, 1/2– 3/5 inch (13–15 mm) long.

3 **Rove beetle.**
Order Coleoptera, family
Staphylinidae (unidentified species)

Rove beetles come in a wide variety
of sizes and shapes, but most are long
and narrow like this one and either
brownish or blackish in color.

4 **Shining fungus beetle.**
Order Coleoptera, family
Staphylinidae, *Scaphidium piceum*
(Melsheimer)

This rotund but very streamlined
rove beetle occurs and feeds on
bracket (or shelf) fungus on old
rotting logs. Other members of its
subgroup feed on various other kinds
of fungi, including mushrooms and
slime molds.

5 Rove beetle.
Order Coleoptera, family
Staphylinidae, *Lathrobium*
(unidentified species)

Species of *Lathrobium* live in damp
areas—near streams, along pond
edges, or in marshes—hiding among
leaves and feeding on small insects or
other invertebrates.

6 Burying beetle.
Order Coleoptera, family Silphidae,
Nicrophorus tomentosus (Weber)

Typically, a male-female pair of
burying beetles, or sexton beetles,
buries a small dead mammal or bird
in the soil to provide food for their
offspring larvae. Pairs of the species
shown here, however, just dig a small
hole and cover the carcass with leaves
and twigs. *Nicrophorus tomentosus*
(1/2–7/10 inch, or 12–18 mm, long) is
easy to tell from other species of
burying beetles (genus *Nicrophorus*)
by the yellow fuzz on its pronotum
(the part between the head and the
black-and-red-striped wing covers).

7 Rove beetle.
Order Coleoptera, family
Staphylinidae, *Platydracus zonatus*
(Gravenhorst)

This species is much smaller than
P. maculosus, only reaching about 3/4
inch (20 mm) long, and is found more
commonly in leaf litter.

8 Rove beetle.
Order Coleoptera, family
Staphylinidae, *Platydracus violaceus.*
(Gravenhorst)

This purplish *Platydracus* species
is most commonly found under the
bark of rotting logs in forests. Adults
are about 1 inch (25 mm) long.

9 Rove beetle.
Order Coleoptera, family
Staphylinidae, *Ontholestes cingulatus*
(Gravenhorst)

This handsome, golden-tailed beetle
occurs mainly in forests and woodlands, where it darts around well
camouflaged in the leaf litter on the
ground. Adults and larvae feed on
insects and other small animals, often
around carrion or dung.

10 Rove beetle.
Order Coleoptera, family
Staphylinidae (unidentified species)

There are so many different kinds
of rove beetles, often so small that
they can be very difficult to identify.
Figures 10–14 depict five little rove
beetles, all no more than 1/5 inch
long!

11 Rove beetle.
Order Coleoptera, family Staphylinidae, *Olophrum obtectum* (Erickson)

This northeastern species is unusually broad-bodied for a rove beetle
and also has relatively long elytra
(wing covers); it is about 1/6 inch
long (4 mm). Little is known about
its habits, but it seems to prefer
slightly damp places.

12 Rove beetle.
Order Coleoptera, family
Staphylinidae, *Omalium rivulare*
(Paykull)

Omalium rivulare is a very widespread species, occurring in Europe,
western Asia, and at least twenty-
four U.S. states and five Canadian
provinces. It is most often associated
with decaying animals, plants, or
fungi. Both adults and larvae apparently eat live or dead small insects
and perhaps other invertebrates, but
may also feed on the decaying material in which they live. Adults are
about 1/7–1/6 inch (3.5–4 mm) long .

13 Rove beetle.
Order Coleoptera, family
Staphylinidae, *Lesteva pallipes*
(LeConte)

This beetle is an eastern United
States and Canadian species that lives
mostly in wooded areas, especially
along the banks of streams, but it has
also been found in caves. Adults are
about 1/7 inch (3.5 mm) long.

14 **Rove beetle.**
Order Coleoptera, family
Staphylinidae, *Thoracophorus costalis*
(Erichson)

This little midget (under 1/10 inch
long) lives in forests in rotting logs
and in leaf litter, where it feeds on
decaying wood, leaves, and tiny fungi.
Its species name, "*costalis*," refers to
the many raised ridges ("costae" in
Latin) on its body surface.

15 **American carrion beetle.**
Order Coleoptera, family Silphidae,
Necrophila americana (2) (Linnaeus)

This large species (15–20 mm long)
is very abundant in all of the eastern
United States and Canada, including
Illinois. In most carrion beetle
species, only the adults move around
actively (females lay their eggs on or
near a source of food for their larvae),
but in this species both adults and
larvae roam about, seeking the carrion on which they depend.

16 **Rove beetle.**
Order Coleoptera, family
Staphylinidae, *Philonthus thoracicus*
(Gravenhorst)

This is a very common species in
Illinois, one of the 112 species of the
large genus *Philonthus* that occur in
North America. Some individuals
of *P. thoracicus* have normal, fully
developed wings and others have
such short wings that they are
unable to fly.

17 **Carrion beetle.**
Order Coleoptera, family Silphidae,
Necrodes surinamensis (Fabricius)

This giant beetle, up to 1-1/10 inch
(28 mm) long, occurs over most of the
United States and southern Canada,
breeding only in large carcasses. They
are active at night and are attracted
to lights. Only males have the enlarged and curved hind legs shown
here.

18 **Rove beetle.**
Order Coleoptera, family Staphylinidae, *Stenus* (unidentified species)

This big-eyed rove beetle is one of
the 2,000 species of *Stenus* known
worldwide. They use their large eyes
for hunting active prey, usually near
streams. If they fall onto the water,
members of some species can skim
quickly along the surface by using
secretions from a special gland near
their tail end.

PLATE XXI

Long-horned Beetles

Long-horned beetles are very diverse and beautiful, and are therefore popular to study. They are attracted to light and can be caught in flight intercept traps and pitfall traps. All can be pests, such as the Asian longhorned beetle. Since nearly all depend on woody plants as larval food, they are found in or near forests, but many adults can be found on flowers, feeding on nectar and pollen.

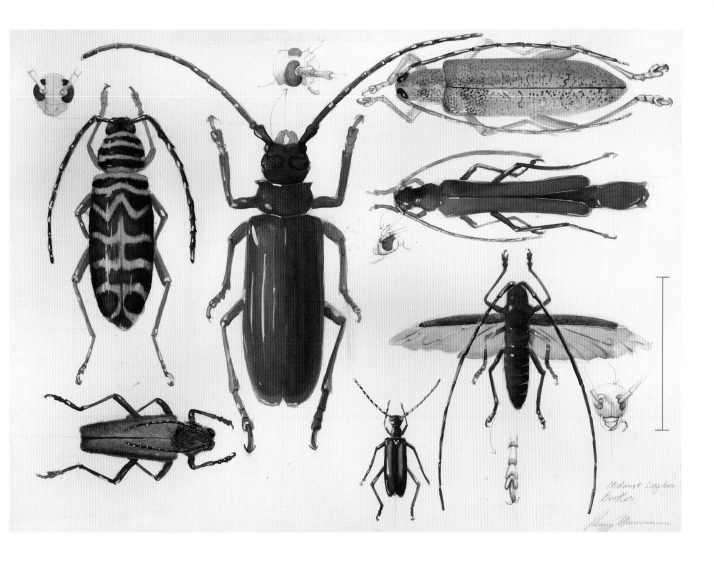

Midwest Longhorn
beetles

[signature]

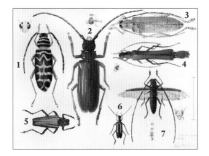

1 **Locust borer.**
Order Coleoptera, family Cerambycidae, *Megacyllene robiniae* (Forster)

The locust borer is one of the best-known longhorns, and is commonly found on goldenrod flowers. Larvae mine in heartwood of black locust and yellow locust.

2 **Brown prionid.**
Order Coleoptera, family Cerambycidae, *Orthosoma brunneum* (Forster)

The brown prionid is a common long-horned beetle that is nocturnal and attracted to lights. It has slender antennae and elongate, weakly ridged wings. Larvae feed in moist, decaying hardwoods and conifers.

3 **Poplar borer.**
Order Coleoptera, family Cerambycidae, *Saperda calcarata* (Say)

The poplar borer is the largest species in the genus *Saperda*, with distinct spines at the wing tips and long antennae. Males have elongated forelegs and expanded, fringed tarsi. Females lay eggs in slits they cut in the bark, usually near the middle portion of trees. Color varies, but is usually pastel. Larvae feed in poplars and willows.

4 **Long-horned beetle.**
Order Coleoptera, family Cerambycidae, *Bellamira scalaris* (Say)

This distinctive large species has a short head and pronounced neck; body and elytra are bottle-shaped and variably marked. Males have an expanded abdominal tip. Adults eat pollen and are found in flowers, and are attracted to ultraviolet lights. Larvae feed in decaying hardwoods and pine.

5 **Long-horned beetle.**
Order Coleoptera, family Cerambycidae, *Cosmosalia chrysocoma* (Kirby)

Adults have flat, metallic, golden
elytral hairs and long antennae, and
often resemble bees or wasps. They
feed on pollen and are usually found
on flowers. Larvae feed in decaying
conifers and hardwoods.

6 **Long-horned beetle.**
Order Coleoptera, family Cerambycidae, *Strangalepta abbreviata* (Germar)

Species varies, with black or pale
elytra (wing covers), most commonly
with an abbreviated pale stripe. It has
a round pronotum with short hairs.
Larvae feed in decaying conifers and
hardwoods.

7 **White-spotted sawyer.**
Order Coleoptera, family Cerambycidae, *Monochamus scutellatus* (Say)

This long-horned beetle has wing
covers that are shiny black beneath
short hairs; these are dark and easily
rubbed off in males. Females have
more white patches than males.
Larvae feed in dead and dying
conifers, especially pine.

PLATE XXII

Wasps and Bees

Hymenopterans, the "membrane-winged" insects, include bees, ants, and a large number of other insect taxa referred to as wasps. The Hymenoptera include examples of social insects, such as honeybees and true ants; these insects have developed regimented social systems in which females are divided into worker and queen castes. Such social Hymenoptera may live together in nests or hives of many thousands of individuals, all descended from a single queen. Not all Hymenoptera are social, however; many live a solitary life, coming together only for a brief mating. Less well known are the many families of parasitoid wasps that lay eggs in living hosts, often other insects. These hatch into larvae that feed on the host's tissues before emerging. Such treatment typically kills the host; parasitoids are attracting interest as natural controls on insect pests.

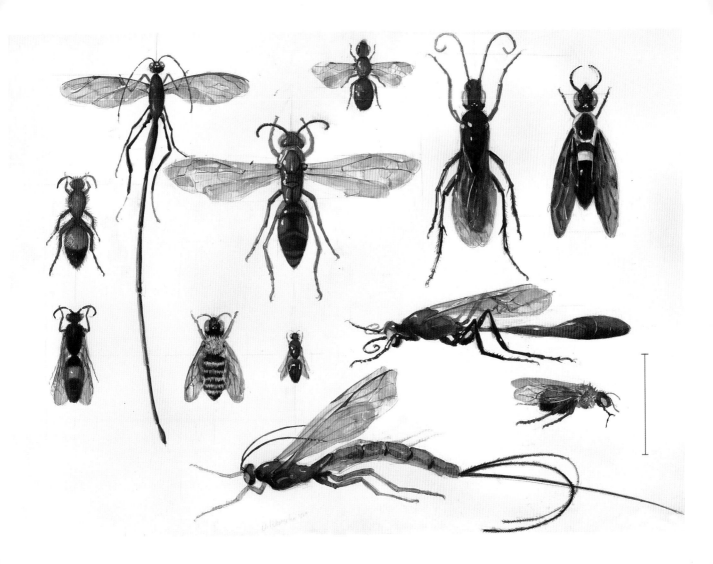

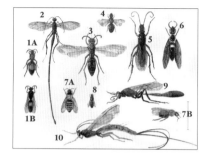

1 **Velvet ant.**
Order Hymenoptera, family Mutillidae, *Dasymutilla* (unidentified species)

Wingless female mutillid wasps (figure 1A) look like colorful, fuzzy ants, but they are not closely related to ants. Winged males (figure 1B) often look quite different from the females. Females wander in open areas with sparse vegetation, often in direct sun. *Dasymutilla* are parasitoids of wasps and bees that nest in the ground and are known for their painful stings. Their bright, gaudy colors advertise to potential predators that they should leave these wingless female wasps alone.

2 **Wasp.**
Order Hymenoptera, family Pelecinidae, *Pelecinus polyturator* (Drury)

These unusual parasitic wasps are not encountered frequently, but generate much excitement when detected. The long tail looks menacing but is only an adaptation in the female for searching out the larvae of May beetles (Scarabaeidae *Phyllophaga* spp.), which are the hosts for this species.

3 **Paper wasp.**
Order Hymenoptera, family Vespidae
(hornets, yellowjackets, potter wasps,
and paper wasps), *Polistes*
(unidentified species)

Vespid wasps are a diverse group of
social and solitary wasps with many
behavioral patterns. *Polistes* is a social
wasp that lives in relatively small
colonies. These colonies are started
when a mated queen begins to build
a nest in the spring. She constructs
her nest from wood fibers that are
chewed and mixed with saliva. The
resultant pulp is then fashioned into
a shelf-like structure with a row of
cells on the bottom side. The queen
cares for the first brood of young by
feeding them nectar and insect prey
such as caterpillars. The offspring
are all infertile females, which then
assume responsibility for feeding the
young and expanding the nest. At this
point, the queen can devote her full
time to laying eggs. Home owners
often find paper-wasp nests under
eaves, in attics, and even under
fence railings.

4 **Cuckoo wasp.**
Order Hymenoptera, family Chrysidi-
dae, *Chrysis* (unidentified species)

Although most go unnoticed because
of their small size, cuckoo wasps are
among the jewels of the hymenopter-
ous insects. Typically, they have
bright metallic colors on a textured
cuticle (insect skin). Their common
name is taken from the habits of
cuckoo birds because the females of
some species lay their eggs in the
nests of other insects, particularly
bees and other wasps. When they
emerge, the larvae steal food from
the host larvae. This unusual behavior is called *kleptoparasitism*. Other
cuckoo wasps are endoparasitoids —
parasitoids that live for a time as
parasites inside another insect but
eventually kill the host. *Chrysis* wasps
are known to be parasitoids of the
larvae of some sphecid wasps.
A most unusual example of para-
sitism from an Asian species of *Chrysis* illustrates how complicated and
elegant nature can be in species
survival. A female *Chrysis* searches
out the nests of its wasp host. She is
followed by another species of parasitic wasp called *Eurytoma*. After the
female *Chrysis* punctures the host

larva and injects an egg, the female
Eurytoma uses the injection site to lay
her own eggs in the same host. *Eurytoma* then becomes a kleptoparasite,
stealing the food source of the developing *Chrysis* larva, and a parasitoid.

5 **Spider wasp.**
Order Hymenoptera, family Pompili-
dae, *Priocnemioides unifasciatus* (Say)

The pompilids, or spider wasps,
contain some of the largest wasps in
the United States. They can often be
seen searching the ground for spiders
or feeding in flowers. Typically, females excavate a burrow in the earth
and provision it with a spider. A
single egg is deposited on the paralyzed spider, which is consumed by
the developing wasp. *Priocnemioides
unifasciatus* is found throughout the
eastern half of the United States and
appears to prefer abandoned fields
and the edges of woodlands.

6 Potter wasp, or mason wasp.

Order Hymenoptera, family Vespidae,
Monobia quadridens (Linnaeus)

The common name of this wasp
group derives from the use of mud
in nest-building by most species.
Females of *Monobia quadridens* bore
tunnels in trees and stems. There
they deposit several eggs, providing
each with a store of several caterpillars. Each chamber is then sealed
off with a mud cap.

One of the marvels of the potter
wasp, and other bees and wasps with
similar habits, is the precise timing
that is required for the successful
emergence of their larvae. When a
series of eggs is deposited single file
in a narrow tunnel and each succes-
sively sealed in, a potential problem
is created: if the first egg were to
mature first, it would be trapped
inside by its siblings on top of it.
Hatching order becomes a matter
of survival. Several strategies are
employed by the female to ensure
that her last eggs mature first. Sex
determination is probably the primary solution to this problem. Since
females take longer to develop than

males, eggs destined to become
female are laid first, male eggs last.
Sex determination in Hymenoptera is
quite simple: fertilized eggs always
become females, unfertilized eggs
male. The female can control which
of her eggs will be fertilized and
which will not. Thus, stem-nesting
wasps tend to have nests with males
toward the end of the stem, and
females at the base.

7 Leafcutting bee.

Order Hymenoptera, family
Megachilidae, *Megachile* (unidentified
species)

This bee is named for its habit of
cutting circular patches from leaves,
which it uses to line the sides of its
nest. These solitary leafcutting bees
make their nests as tunnels in the
ground or in wood. They are different from most bees in that they carry
pollen on the underside of their
abdomen rather than on their hind
legs. (Figures 7A and 7B show a top
and side view, respectively.)

8 Sweat bee.

Order Hymenoptera, family
Halictidae, *Augochloropsis metallica*
(Fabricius)

Halictid bees, called "sweat bees,"
tend to be the most common of the
bees. Unlike the social honey bees,
most other types of bees, including
the sweat bees (with rare exceptions),
are solitary and don't live in colonies.
Their common name is derived from
their habit of licking the sweat from
other animals, including humans.
Their purpose is strictly benign with
no ill intent. A sting results only if a
bee accidentally gets trapped next
to the skin. Most halictids make
nests in the ground by digging a
number of tunnels. *Augochloropsis
metallica* places several larval chambers in close association with each
other. Each chamber is provided
with a food mass consisting mostly
of pollen. An egg is placed on the
food mass and sealed into the
chamber.

9 Thread-waisted wasp.

Order Hymenoptera, family Spheci-
dae, *Ammophila* (unidentified species)

Sphecid wasps are a diverse family
of predaceous solitary wasps. Most
construct nests by digging cavities
in the ground. They often demonstrate a strong preference in the prey
they feed their young. *Ammophila*
specialize in hunting caterpillars. As
is usually the case in solitary wasps
that provide animal food for their
young, the prey are stung and not
killed. The venom is meant to para-
lyze the caterpillar, which eventually
meets its end by being devoured.
Dead prey would quickly decompose
and limit the amount of food available to the growing wasp; and fungi
and bacteria growing on the dead
prey might pose a health hazard to
the young developing wasp.

10 **Ichneumon wasp.**

Order Hymenoptera, family
Ichneumonidae, *Dolichomitus irritator*
(Fabricius)

The Ichneumonidae is a diverse
family of endoparasitic wasps that
attack a variety of insect hosts.
The name derives from an Egyptian
mongoose, which preys on, among
other things, the eggs and young of
crocodiles. Likewise, these wasps
search out the eggs and larvae of
other insects into which they lay
their eggs. The larvae then live as
parasitoids (an insect and especially a
wasp that completes its larval development by feeding on the body of
another insect, eventually killing it,
and is free-living as an adult). Many
Ichneumonids are natural enemies of
pest insects, for example, *D. irritator*
attacks the larvae of a destructive
weevil called the "poplar-and-willow
borer," *Cryptorhynchus lapathi* (Linnaeus). A lot of research goes into
finding and using such parasitoids to
control pest insects that are accidentally introduced into the United
States. This requires searching for
parasitoids in the pests' homeland-
sand doing extensive experimental
work to ensure that introducing
them will not harm populations
of our native insects.

PLATE XXIII

Wasp Nests

The ancient Romans referred to wasps and hornets by the word *vespa*. This word enters English in its corrupted Anglo-Saxon form, *waesp*. Illinois social wasps belong to the family Vespidae, which includes the paper wasps, hornets, and yellowjackets. Not all vespids are social, however; the family contains many solitary forms such as the potter wasps.

In the spring, social vespids make nesting material from woody fibers that are scraped from living plants or wooden buildings. This is chewed into a pulp and laid down in strips. The inner nest consists of a flat shelf with many chambers, or cells, that face downward. In hornets and yellowjackets, an outer envelope of this papery material is constructed over these shelves. As the population of the nest increases, more shelves are added below the older ones. The queen lays an egg in each of these cells

actual
size

Wasps nest
(rodent) wasp &
hornet

and cares for the developing larvae by feeding them chewed insects, which she hunts. After the first generation of wasps mature, the queen devotes her full time to laying eggs, leaving child rearing, hunting, and other chores to the young wasps.

By fall the wasps begin to produce special cells that contain the males and the queens of the following year. At this time the nest population stops growing and larvae may even be cannibalized or discarded. The worker females begin to lose their social instinct and gradually abandon the nest. The new queens mate and look for a place to overwinter. Each starts her own nest in the spring. The nonreproductive population of the nest dies, with the onset of killing frosts. Nests quickly disintegrate and are not used again.

Vespid wasps, like all other Hymenoptera, are haplodiploid, that is, females have two sets of chromosomes (and so are diploid) while the males only have one (and are thus haploid). It follows that all fertilized eggs are female and unfertilized eggs are male.

It has been observed that aggressiveness in yellowjackets and paper wasps tends to increase toward late summer. Research seems to indicate that this may have a lot to do with the critical period when reproductives (males and future queens) are produced in the nest. The success of a colony can be measured by its success in producing new fertile queens. Protecting this investment is critical to species survival. Similar aggressiveness has been observed in other colonial insects such as aphids, fire ants, and termites.

Aggression toward humans, as with most wasps, is nearly always the result of disturbing their nests, which they prefer to keep away from human traffic. The benefits of tolerating their presence far outweigh our perceived threats from them. The success of Illinois gardens is due in part, perhaps a large part, to their predatory habits.

The circled figures show sizes scaled to the 1 inch line. The others are enlarged, except figure 1B, which is reduced.

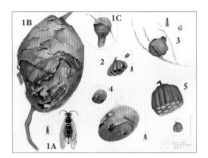

1 **Bald-faced hornet.**
Order Hymenoptera, family Vespidae,
Dolichovespula maculata (Linnaeus)

This species is Illinois' largest
hornet (figure 1A), a fact that often
causes undue alarm to people who
encounter them. For the most part,
bald-faced hornets are benign when
they share living space with humans.
They typically make their nests in
trees where the foliage hides their
presence. Frequently, homeowners
in urban areas only become aware of
their presence in autumn when leaf-
fall reveals their nests. *Dolichovespula
maculata* hunt for living food—
mostly other insects and even other
kinds of yellowjackets. Their nests
(figure 1B) are usually the size of
a football and contain about 250
adults. This plate also depicts the
initial stage of the nest (figure 1C),
which is constructed by the queen.
These queen nests often have
long entrance tunnels.

2 **Red paper wasp.**
Order Hymenoptera, family Vespidae,
Polistes annularis (Linnaeus)

Unlike yellowjacket nests, paper-
wasp nests consist of a single shelf
that is not covered by a protective
envelope. There seems to be a great
versatility in the fate of future queens
in *P. annularis*. Some may begin their
own colonies as the sole queen. Others may begin colonies in a group and
become the dominant queen while
the others become secondary queens.
It has been noted that this species
is less tolerant of intrusions near its
nests. This may explain why the red
paper wasp prefers to live in rural
areas.

3 **Potter wasp.**
Order Hymenoptera, family Vespidae,
Eumenes verticalis Say

The potter wasp represents a
solitary member of the family Vespidae. Unlike the social yellowjackets
and paper wasps, members of the
genus *Emenes* construct their tiny,
jug-like nests out of mud. A female
lays a single egg in each jug and pro-
ceeds to fill it with paralyzed caterpillars. Several of these jugs may be
attached in a row to a twig.

4 **Common yellowjacket.**
Order Hymenoptera, family Vespidae,
Vespula vulgaris (Linnaeus)

The common yellowjacket is found
in Europe and the United States. It
generally forms nests underground
with colonies commonly exceeding
500 individuals. The notoriety of this
species and its near relatives derives
from its habit of scavenging at carrion and garbage cans. *Vespula vulgaris* is a common pest at parks and
a frequent interloper at human
recreational activities.

5 **Paper wasp.**
Order Hymenoptera, family Vespidae,
Polistes fuscatus (Fabricius)

A small comb of *P. fuscatus* illustrates
how each cell is sealed when the larva
matures. Pupation is completed in
the sealed chamber and the emerging
adult wasp must chew its way to
freedom.

PLATE XXIV

Millipedes and Centipedes

The centipedes and millipedes are mostly soil dwellers. Superficially, they may look similar, but they have very different life styles. Most millipedes are vegetarians, chewing on decaying leaves from the previous fall. They are very important to the health of Illinois forests because they help in the decomposition of leaves. Centipedes, on the other hand, are all predators, hunting among the leaf litter, in the soil, and under logs for smaller animals to feed on. Both centipedes and millipedes have long bodies with many, many legs. The longest one is a millipede species with 375 pairs of legs. Millipedes and centipedes differ in the arrangement of their legs: centipedes have one pair of legs attached to each of their body rings (segments), while millipedes have two pairs of legs at each ring.

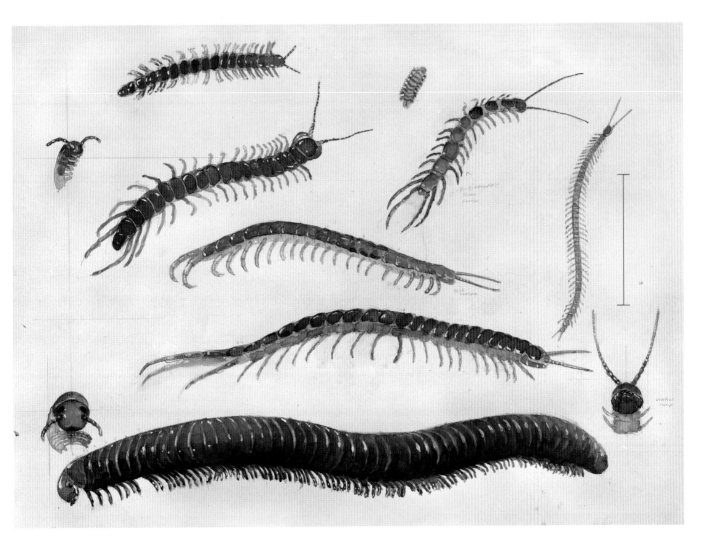

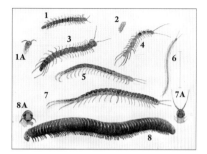

1 **Hothouse millipede.**
Order Polydesmida, family Paradoxo-
somatidae, *Oxidus gracilis* (Koch)

This polydesmid millipede, not yet
fully grown, is a long way from home.
This species came from Japan and
first occurred in North American
greenhouses. Figure 1A is a head study
for figure 1. Millipedes hatch from
eggs with very few legs. As they grow
and molt, rings are added to the body.
The older the millipede, the more
legs it will have. Many millipede
species live in the forest litter where
they feed on decaying leaves. They
often rest under fallen tree trunks.
Some species feed on rotting wood
and can be found under the bark of
tree trunks.

2 **Bristle millipede.**
Order Pselaphognatha, family
Polyxenidae (unidentified species)

The bristle millipede is the smallest
of the millipedes (0.1 inch, or 3 mm).
Its body is covered with long, strong
bristles. It lives in the deeper layers
of the forest floor. Two families,
comprised of 60 species, can be
found all over the world.

3 **Centipede.**
Order Scolopendromorpha, family
Scolopocryptopidae, *Scolopocryptops*
(unidentified species)

All Scolopendromorpha have between 21 and 23 pairs of legs. Juveniles
have fewer legs. The antennae have
between 17 and 30 segments. They
are mainly tropical, but some species
of the families Scolopocryptopidae
and Cryptopidae are found in Illinois. They can be quite venomous
and, when caught in the hand, they
bite.

4 **Stone centipede.**
Order Lithobiomorpha, family
Lithobiidae (unidentified species)

Stone centipedes all have 15 pairs of
legs when fully grown. They can be
found under rocks and live in yards.

5 **Centipede.**
Order Scolopendromorpha, family Scolopendridae, *Hemiscolopendra marginaria* (Say)

This beautiful centipede was collected in a forest in Southern Illinois.

6 **Soil centipede.**
Order Geophilomorpha, family Geophilidae (unidentified species)

Soil centipedes are blind. They have between 31 and 177 pairs of legs, and each leg can move independently. They hunt for small prey and live very deep in the soil.

7 **Centipede.**
Order Scolopendromorpha, family Scolopendridae (unidentified species)

This large, handsome centipede has 21 pairs of legs. Some of its relatives are very large and aggressive. Figure 7A is a head study for figure 7. The underside of the centipede's head shows its poison fangs. Centipedes have very long antennae.

8 **Millipede.**
Order Spirobolida, family Spirobolidae, *Narceus americanus* (Beauvois)

This is the largest millipede in Illinois woods and a native of North America. It can be found coiled up in or under logs, where it eats wood and leaves. If held in a closed hand, it emits chemicals through its pores, which can cause a chemical burn and stain skin red. The millipedes use these secretions to deter predators. If you let it crawl around, it is harmless. Figure 8A is a head study for figure 8. Like all millipedes, *N. americanus* has two short antennae and two areas with many small eyes grouped together.

PLATE XXV

Spiders

These elegant, eight-legged animals are all hunters, catching live prey in fine silken webs, or hunting in the vegetation and among the rich leaf litter of an Illinois oak savanna. Illinois prairies with tall grasses and bushes offer attractive "web sites" for spiders to make their homes and set their traps. They spend the long winters as hatchlings in a safe silken cocoon, or as teenagers hidden deep in crevices, under bark and in the soil. Despite their predatory lifestyle, nearly all spiders are harmless to humans; a spider bites only in self-defense.

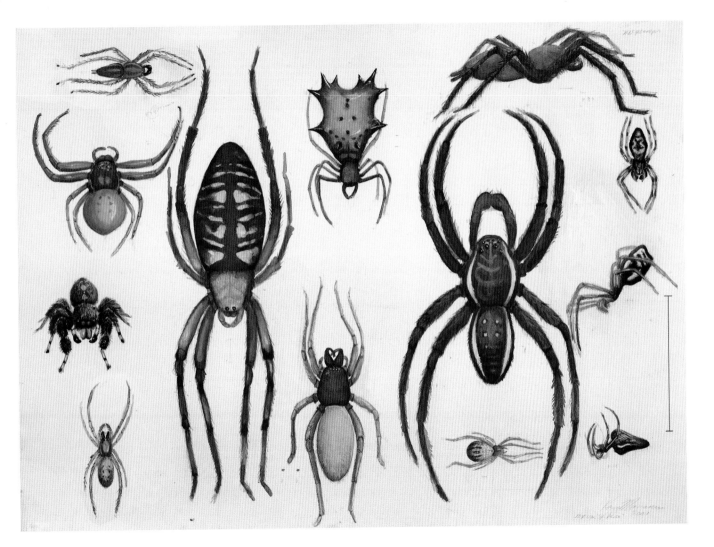

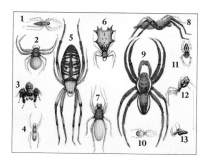

2 Goldenrod crab spider.
Order Araneae, family Thomisidae,
Misumena vatia (Clerck)

These small spiders are ambush predators. They wait patiently in flowers
holding their powerful front legs open
to catch unsuspecting nectar seekers.
Members of this group are often
brightly colored—green, yellow, white,
and pink—matching the color of their
flower; some can even change color.

4 Orb-weaving spider.
Order Araneae, family Araneidae,
Larinia directa (Hentz)

Whereas many orb weavers have
short legs and a round abdomen,
Larinia spiders have long legs and
an elongated abdomen. This species
hunts in its oblique orb-web at night,
hanging in the center, or hub, of the
web. During the day, they hide in
vegetation next to the web.

1 Grass spider.
Order Araneae, family Agelenidae,
Agelenopsis potteri (Blackwall)

Beginning in the early summer you
can find this spider's triangular sheet
web in bushes and in the grass. Each
triangular sheet ends in a funnel into
which the spider quickly retreats if it
senses danger.

3 Jumping spider.
Order Araneae, family Salticidae,
Phidippus audax (Hentz)

Members of this large family of
spiders are spectacular leapers. They
are heavy bodied and pounce on their
insect prey. Mantisfly females (Mantispidae; see plate XII, figure 4)
sometimes lay eggs in the egg sac of
the jumping spider. The mantispid
larvae eat the spider eggs and emerge
as adults out of the spider egg sac.
Usually they leave 2–3 spider eggs and
the spider population is not adversely
affected.

5 Black-and-yellow garden spider.
Order Araneae, family Araneidae,
Argiope aurantia (Lucas)

The largest spider you may ever see,
the strikingly colored garden spider
hangs head down in its large, vertical
orb web. In the fall, impressively
large gravid females may frighten the
casual observer. These spiders produce a delicate but durable silken
egg sac from which spiderlings hatch
the following spring. They prefer tall
prairie grasses for their large webs.
If you haven't mowed your yard in a
while, you may have given an Illinois
native a perfect home.

6 Spiny orb weaver.
Order Araneae, family Araneidae,
Micrathena gracilis (Walckenaer)

These spiny orb weavers make perfectly round, very fine, and even-meshed webs in the Illinois woods. The females make a perfect new web every day, recycling the valuable silk from last night's web by eating it. The males of this species are tiny.

7 Wood louse eater.
Order Araneae, family Dysderidae,
Dysdera crocata C. L. Koch

A recent immigrant from Europe, this spider is common in Illinois gardens. They hide under rocks and logs. They use their long fangs to catch wood lice (isopods). In contrast to most other spiders on this plate, *Dysdera* lives for several years.

8 Yellow sac spider.
Order Araneae, family Clubionidae,
Cheiracanthium mildei L. Koch

The yellow sac spider occurs mostly in houses in this country. It has been implicated in somewhat painful spider bites. It hunts insects, usually at night. It spends the day in silken tube-like retreats that look like sacs. It occurs outdoors in warmer regions, such as the Mediterranean countries.

9 Six-spotted fishing spider.
Order Araneae. Family Pisauridae,
Dolomedes triton (Walckenaer)

Courageous hunters and patient fishermen, these spiders rest their front legs on slow-flowing waters, hidden by overhanging vegetation of the embankment and catch everything that fits their size. Mothers carry their silken egg sac around with them and build a nursery web for the first week of their hatchlings' lives.

10 Lined orb weaver.
Order Araneae. Family Araneidae,
Mangora gibberosa (Hentz)

This small orb weaver makes its fine-meshed webs in the grass, or in the understory of woods. It builds no retreat, but hangs in the hub of the web. When disturbed, the spider runs quickly to the outside of the web and down the vegetation or drops from the center of the web by a silken thread.

11 Striped lynx spider.
Order Araneae, family Oxyopidae,
Oxyopes salticus Hentz

This spider is an active hunter during the day and does not make webs to capture prey. It gets within reach of its prey then assumes a specific pose, raising and extending the long front legs before it leaps on its prey. This species is one of the most common in tall grasses and herbaceous vegetation. Especially from mid-June to September, lynx spiders are extremely abundant and are the main predators of insects living in grassy and weedy fields.

12 Bowl-and-doily spider.
Order Araneae, family Linyphiidae,
Frontinella communis (Hentz)

This spider is very plentiful around Illinois woods and gardens. It builds almost invisible, fine silken webs, a horizontal sheet with a scaffolding above the sheet. This web architecture inspired the spider's common name, the bowl-and-doily spider. Insects flying into the scaffolding fall down onto the sheet. The spider hangs beneath the sheet and attacks the prey from below.

13 Trashline orb weaver.
Order Aaneae, family Araneidae,
Cyclosa conica (Pallas)

Building webs high up under eaves, these spiders spend their time in the hub of their webs, camouflaged by debris they arrange in a vertical line in the web.

PLATE XXVI

Spiders and Their Webs

All spiders have silk glands in their abdomen (the hind body part) and spinnerets, which have spigots to release the silk. Spiders make more than one kind of silk. Different silk glands produce sticky silk for prey capture, strong dragline silk (not sticky), attachment threads, core fibers for sticky silk, swathing silk to wrap prey, and soft silk for the inside of the egg sac. Nearly all spiders use silk as a protection for their eggs. Many spiders build retreats for molting. Spiders usually wear "safety belts" when running about: a thread of strong silk is attached to the substrate from time to time and silk is released continuously. Should the spider need to jump to safety, its life literally hangs on a thread of silk. About half of the 37,000 spider species in the world use silk for prey capture. They build a variety

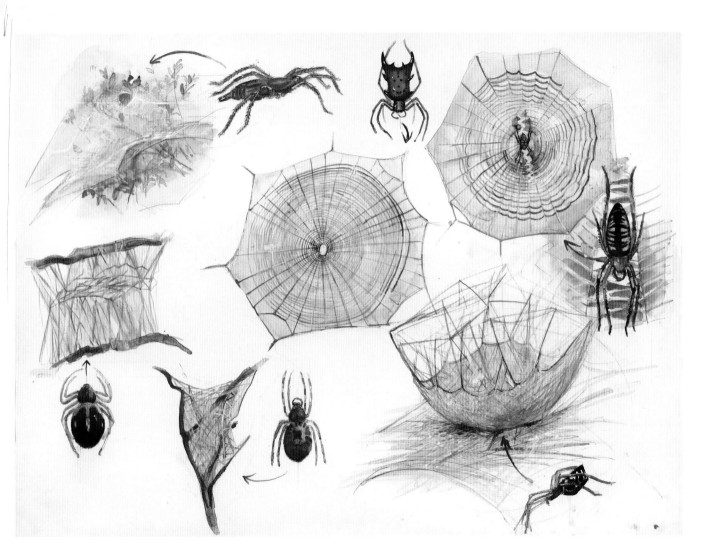

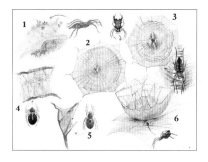

of different silken traps, as illustrated here on the spiders' web page, to make a living. The other half of spider species hunt their prey by other means—on the surface of the water, waiting in ambush in flowers, or by searching through vegetation.

1 **Funnel web of a grass spider.**
Order Araneae, family Agelenidae, *Agelenopsis* (unidentified species)

Toward the end of summer and into the fall, the funnel webs of the grass spiders (*Agelenopsis*) can be found covered with dew in the early morning. Webs are built on lawns and in bushes, and can often be found around yards and gardens. The spiders usually wait in the entrance of the funnel, poised to rush out to catch any insects scrambling over the silken sheet web. The spiders quickly retreat deep into the funnel when frightened or disturbed. Prey is also carried into the funnel to be eaten. Seven different species of the genus *Agelenopsis* make their home in Illinois.

2 **Orb web of a spiny orb weaver.**
Order Araneae, family Araneidae, *Micrathena gracilis* (Walckenaer)

The fine-meshed orb webs of the spiny orb weaver (*Micrathena gracilis*) have many radii and a dense, sticky spiral. The *Micrathena* orb web is often built at an angle, with the spider hanging upside down in the open hub of the web. These spiders prefer wooded areas and are active during the day. The threads of the spiral of the orb web are covered with moist glue and are very thin and difficult to see, especially for flying insects. Three species of spiny orb weavers live in Illinois; the majority of their relatives prefer warmer climates.

3 **Orb web of a black-and-yellow garden spider.**
Order Araneae, family Araneidae, *Argiope aurantia* (Lucas)

The colorful spiders of this genus are large and conspicuous, especially in the fall, when females are fully grown and carry a lot of eggs in their abdomen (hind body part). The orb web of *Argiope* is perfectly vertical, and the spider "writes" in its web—broad, silken zigzag bands extend upward and downward from the hub. *Argiope* makes its web in the tall grasses of the prairies, waiting during the day for insects to fly into the web. The spider tightly wraps its prey in silk, then spends time eating, while remaining in its hub. Because of the damage done to the web during prey capture, the spider takes the web down and recycles its silk by eating it. A new orb web is put up within an hour.

4 **Gum-footed tangle web of a cobweb spider.**
Order Araneae, family Theridiidae, *Steatoda borealis* (Hentz)

Cobweb spiders make their capture webs in dark, low places around rocks and logs. The spider stays close by the web (but not in it) while waiting for prey. The silk lines extending to the ground are studded with glue droplets. This spider hunts walking, rather than flying, insect prey. The genus is distributed worldwide; five of its species live in Illinois. They are related to the black widow spiders and the house cobweb spiders.

5 **Hackle-band web of a hackle-band spider.**
Order Araneae, family Dictynidae, *Dictyna* (unidentified species)

This group of hackle-band spiders resembles the cobweb weavers. They build irregular webs usually at the tips of tall plants, but also under leaves and in crevices. These spiders use a special type of trapping silk. The silken threads that catch prey are covered not in moist glue but in extremely fine wool-like silk. The spiny legs of insects become entangled in this natural "velcro-style" sticky silk. As there is no moist glue to dry up, hackle-band webs catch prey longer and do not need to be replaced as often.

6 **Web of a bowl-and-doily spider.**
Order Araneae, family Linyphiidae, *Frontinella communis* (Hentz)

Most members of this family are very small. The bowl-and-doily spider is famous for its complex web. The spider hangs upside down below the bowl-shaped sheet and above the "doily." When a flying insect becomes entangled in the silken scaffolding and falls into the "bowl," the spider bites its prey from below the sheet. There is no glue on the threads of this web, so the spider has to catch its prey quickly. Webs of the bowl-and-doily spider can be found in many natural and human-altered Illinois habitats. *Frontinella communis* has many relatives in the area: as many as 204 species of sheet web spiders are known to be throughout the Midwest, many of them in Illinois.

PLATE XXVII   *Drawings of a Living Mantid*

Chinese Mantid.

Order Mantodea, family Mantidae, *Tenodera aridifolia sinensis* (Saussure)

A note from the artist. One of the most interesting aspects of entomology is the study of live insects. It is hard to keep a bird or mammal in a jar long enough for prolonged observation. With bugs it is easy. After the 2002 Calumet BioBlitz (a "BioBlitz" is a 24-hour survey of one area's biodiversity), Jim Louderman brought a live mantid back to the Field Museum. I spent a couple of days drawing the mantid as it meandered around a glass tank. Having drawn pinned, lifeless insects for years, I found this to be a very rewarding experience. The mantid seemed to be staring at me. I came to look forward to its particular gaze each morning. People actually keep mantids as pets. You can buy crickets at a local pet store and feed them daily. The mantid has binocular vision, which allows this amazing insect to figure the exact distance to its prey, striking in less than 100 milliseconds. The creature moved too fast for me to capture its motion on paper, but I was able to sketch it in various resting poses. Drawing is another way to understand insects—their complexities, the ways they move, and their curious behavior.